THE SIMPLE MATH OF WRITING WELL

Writing for the 21st Century

DR. JENNIE A. HARROP

The Simple Math of Writing Well by Dr. Jennie A. Harrop is licensed under a Creative Commons Attribution-NonCommercial-ShareAlike 4.0 International License, except where otherwise noted.

ISBN: 978-0-9998292-0-2

Attribution-NonCommercial-ShareAlike
CC BY-NC-SA

View License Deed | View Legal Code

Cover by Jamison McAndie | Unsplash

CONTENTS

About the Book   vi

Reviewers' Notes   viii

Preface: Writing as Simple Math   xi
Andragogy & Rule Changes

Introduction: Myths and Rule Changes   1
1 + 1 = 2

PART I. THE SENTENCE EQUATION

1. Main Verbs   18
2. Main Subjects   26
3. Terminal Punctuation Marks   35
4. Mid-Sentence Punctuation Marks   43
5. Eight Parts of Speech   58
6. Consistency   68

PART II. THE PARAGRAPH EQUATION

7. Topic Sentences   79
8. Evidence   84
9. Summary Sentences   89

PART III. THE ESSAY EQUATION

10. Thesis Statements — 96
11. Introductions — 101
12. Body Paragraphs — 107
13. Conclusions — 112

PART IV. THE PROCESS OF WRITING WELL

14. Purpose — 119
15. Audience — 126
16. Voice — 133
17. Context — 140
18. Claims and Appeals — 147
19. Clarity and Cohesion — 154
20. Revision and Creativity — 160

PART V. RESEARCH

21. Finding Credible Evidence — 168
22. Including Outside Evidence — 176

PART VI. ACADEMIC FORMATTING

23. APA — 185
24. MLA — 193
25. Turabian — 200

PART VII. BEYOND ACADEMIA

26.	Emails	209
27.	Letters	214
28.	Reports and Proposals	219
	Conclusion	224
	About the Author	227

ABOUT THE BOOK

Written for students and post-students seeking a reminder of the basic rules of effective writing, *The Simple Math of Writing Well: Writing for the 21st Century* focuses on the mathematical structure of language, pinpointing the differences between essential and inessential rules of writing: Essential rules are necessary to maintain the mathematical patterns we expect – *Use commas to separate items in a list of two or more,* for example. But inessential rules have confused writers for generations – *Use commas sparingly,* for instance, or *Be sure your sentences aren't too long.* Rather than muddling subjective preferences with the essential rules of grammar, *The Simple Math of Writing Well* draws a clear line between the two, empowering writers to be intentional about the choices they make.

While mathematics can be intimidating, the math in this book is refreshingly simple. Just as 1 + 1 = 2, readers will be prodded to recall such elementary equations as *subject + verb = sentence* and *topic sentence + evidence = paragraph.* Harrop divides her discussion of mechanics into logical sections – the Sentence Equation, the Paragraph Equation, and the Essay Equation – followed by chapters addressing effective writing processes, the challenges of research in the Google age, accurate academic formatting, and the netiquette of proper emails, letters, and proposals. The *Simple Math of Writing Well* trains writers to focus on purpose, audience, and voice for all writerly decisions, encouraging them to write with clarity and confidence.

Writing guides abound, but *The Simple Math of Writing Well* is one of a kind. Readers will find its practical approach affirming, encouraging, and informative, and its focus on the basics of linguistic structure releases 21st-century writers to embrace the variety of mediums that define our internet-connected world. As Harrop reminds us in the opening chapters of her book, we write more today than ever before in history: texts, emails, letters, blogs, reports, social media posts, proposals, etc. *The Simple Math of Writing Well* is the first guide that directly addresses the importance of writing well in the Google age.

REVIEWERS' NOTES

LISBETH CHAPIN

Simply put, *The Simple Math of Writing Well* is a breakthrough in writing guides — and in twenty-seven years of teaching writing, I have tried many different strategies and texts. Students today need a new kind of instruction for the environment of technology in which they are immersed, and they need to know that we writing instructors can respond to that with a clear and proven method for the assignments they need to do. *The Simple Math of Writing Well* accomplishes that by combining brief definitions with thorough explanations, followed by exercises that connect concept to practice very effectively. The equations, such as topic sentence + evidence = paragraph, are the kind of simple guide students can grasp while applying those equations to develop complex ideas. Technology has not only changed how students find information but also how they read and think. Dr. Harrop's direct approach responds to that, and *The Simple Math* is what a true writing handbook should be, connecting good writing instruction with the immediacy of application, generating a momentum that students can experience for a greater sense of their own writing agency. I'm recommending it to all our writing instructors.

Dr. Lisbeth Chapin is Associate Professor of English, Writing Program Coordinator, Gwynedd Mercy University, Gwynedd Valley, PA
chapin.L@gmercyu.edu

CHRISTINE GILLETTE

The *Simple Math of Writing Well: Writing in the 21st Century* is a refreshingly clear, thoughtful, and helpful resource for both students and teachers of writing. While designed as a text for a college-level writing course, the book is also highly appropriate as a supplemental writing resource for high school students, college students of any major, or even non-university students who are seeking a refresher on the basics of writing.

Author Jennie A. Harrop presents readers with a lucid, structural philosophy of writing that deftly balances both theory and practice. Particularly noteworthy is Harrop's focus on the difference between essential and inessential rules for writing. Correctly asserting that many of the "rules" for writing ("do not end a sentence with a preposition"; "do not use first-person pronouns") are inessential because they fail to account for the audience, purpose, or rhetorical context of a given writing project, Harrop instead offers readers a set of essential rules that focus on increasing the clarity and developing the meaning of a text. These begin at the sentence level, moving on to paragraphs, then essay structure, and culminate with an examination of the writing process itself.

For too many students, writing classes are the subject of apprehension and frustration precisely because the question of what constitutes "good" writing seems so arbitrary and subjective. *The Simple Math of Writing Well* seeks to dispel these anxieties by offering readers a precise and straightforward guide to writing that demystifies the structure and process of writing while offering a substantial set of tools to help writers craft their work.

Dr. Christine Gillette, Metropolitan State University of Denver

POLLY PETERSON

An excellent choice as the principle book in a writing course or as a supplemental writing text in a discipline-specific class, this book is a brief and complete writing manual with an approachable voice, clear rules, ample examples, and self-directed activities.

The purpose of the book is to demystify writing and breakdown the misconceptions around the rules of grammar and usage. Drawing on her career as a journalist, writing professor, and adult education program director, Harrop uses personal examples to speak to an audience of reluctant writers, demonstrating that writing is not as subjective as people fear. By understanding the simple rules — the mathematics — of grammar and usage, anyone can write well.

The book starts by addressing the myths surrounding grammar usage and punctuation and replacing those false rules with the correct ones. The next three chapters are at the center of Harrop's conceptual metaphor of writing-as-math, turning discourse into equations: the sentence equation, the paragraph equation, the essay equation. The last part of the book presents the writing process, research writing instruction, academic formatting, and writing in the professional world.

The brilliance of this book is in its audience focus: the confused grammarian in all of us. Her simple "1 + 1 = 2" approach to writing makes us confident that we can learn grammar, that we can write better, that we can communicate more clearly. An excellent choice for the classroom or as a reference for anyone who writes.

Polly Peterson is Assistant Professor of English, Director of General Education, at George Fox University

PREFACE: WRITING AS SIMPLE MATH

Andragogy & Rule Changes

If you train your brain to spot the basic structure of language, writing will come as easily as speaking. Just as 1 + 1 = 2, we all naturally anticipate the math equation of a complete sentence, of a well-written paragraph, and of a satisfying essay. Linguists will tell you that our brains are wired for language. Some of us anticipate the equation consciously and some of us subconsciously, but we all recognize when a piece is missing and the language on the page or on the screen just doesn't seem right. The goal of this book is to help you recognize the simple math of effective writing. Once you learn to spot the building blocks, you can be confident that your audience will focus on your content rather than your mechanics.

I realized the importance of the language that swirled in my brain. Without mathematical order, without clarity and simplicity, my readers or listeners – whoever they were – would never see the moments that I had seen. [Image: Sawyer Bengtson | Unsplash]

I pressed my boot against the metal frame of the phone booth's folding door, praying that I could keep it securely closed as I squeezed the receiver to my ear with my shoulder and gripped pepper spray in my right hand and my reporter's notebook in my left. The scraggly-haired man half a block south looked high on something, and I didn't want him barging into the booth while I was running my story. I focused hard on the scrawled notes before me, trying to remember the fire chief's words as he threw the charred space heater through the heat-exploded second floor window of Chicago's Cabrini Green. The nouns and verbs lined up in my brain in orderly patterns, and by the time I hung up the phone and relaxed my foot, I was confident that I had listed every fact, every nuance, every witness account. I had reported that night's story the best that I could.

As I settled into my 1981 Honda, ready to drive back to the Englewood Police Department for my next assignment, I heard the words I had just recited to my editor emerging from Chicago's WGN Radio. I gripped the stick shift and listened somewhat horrified, waiting for the ill-placed pronoun or misconstrued detail. I realized in that moment the importance of the language that swirled in my brain. Without mathematical order, without clarity and simplicity, my readers or listeners – whoever they were – would never see the moments that I had seen.

I was the kid who reveled in the craft of diagramming sentences on the chalkboard in Mrs. Perrin's sixth-grade class – much to my friends' annoyance – but my best linguistic training came on the streets of Chicago's South Side in the early 1990s. When I worked as a crime and news reporter for City News Bureau, a wire service that served as Chicago's journalism boot camp for more than 100 years, there was no time to ponder prepositions or worry about misplaced modifiers when I was braced in a phone booth at 2:30 a.m. And there was no room for error.

The bureau's motto was, "If your mother says she loves you, check it out," and we reporters were trained to think quickly, question thoroughly, and compose efficiently. The publishers of 10 Chicago daily newspapers founded CNB in 1890 to cover police news at night, preventing the regular reporters from wasting their time on false leads. By the 1990s, CNB was a 24-hour crime and news service reporting to dozens of metropolitan and national media outlets, training scores of green journalists with its merciless hard-knocks training. Some of its better-known alumni included *Chicago Tribune* columnist Mike Royko and novelist Kurt Vonnegut.

Thorough evidence was critical. Seasoned reporters told the story of the CNB rookie who covered a toddler's death one Christmas morning. The reporter dutifully questioned family members about how and why the toddler had choked on the shards of a glass Christmas tree ball – undoubtedly a wrenching experience for the rookie. When the reporter finished his phone call with some relief and filed his story, his rewrite editor berated him for neglecting one key detail: the color of the Christmas tree ball. The reporter was forced to call the family back, imposing on their grief with a seemingly inconsequential detail. The lesson? Get it right the first time.

Prewriting was also essential. Yes, it's difficult to prewrite when you have no idea what squawks will emerge from the police scanner, so our assignment was to soak ourselves in news every waking moment: read at least three daily newspapers, two metro and one national, and listen to radio or TV news at every possible moment. My first assignment after I moved to Chicago from the Northwest was to cover a news conference with then-Governor Jim Edgar. My editor told me to simply stay alert and take notes, no questions needed this time, but the veteran reporters from other news agencies spotted my false nonchalance immediately.

As the news conference ended, the press of reporters encircling Edgar pulled back and everyone seemed to look my way at once, smirking condescendingly as one woman asked whether the new City News reporter had any questions for the governor. "Not this time," I said with false bravado. I had moved to Chicago just one week prior, and I knew nothing about Jim Edgar, Jim Thompson, Alan Dixon, or either of the Rich Daleys. Governor Edgar clapped me on the shoulder before he turned away. "Next time, Champ," he said. Next time, indeed. I was in the library for hours the next day researching Illinois history and Chicago politics.

The first time I called in a story by payphone, I wasn't sure what to say. "What do you need first?" I asked the rewrite editor as I stood in the phone booth skimming through my notes. He was not pleased with my question or my inefficiency. "What do you mean?" he screamed into the phone. "Just give me the damn story! This should have gone out minutes ago!" I quickly realized that I didn't have time to compose in the classic sense of the word *composition*. Writing had to become second nature if I was going to survive on those streets. I learned to narrow each new event to a single thesis statement as I stood at the scene, and then seek out the exhaustive evidence that would satisfy even the grouchiest of editors. I learned to recite stories rapidly from pages of illegible scribblings, pulling the most important information to the top and letting the superfluous slide away. I learned to set my ego aside as we rushed to move stories with speed and accuracy.

On more than one occasion, I emerged from a phone booth to hear the story I had just called in being read over the radio in my old Accord. It was humbling, to say the least, to hear the words I had just slung together in a race against time read by someone sitting comfortably in a studio. At first, I wanted to shout excuses at the radio: "I was under too much pressure!" "I didn't have time to think of better verbs!" "The police commander I interviewed wouldn't speak in complete sentences!" But I later realized that it was more about math than craft at this level. If I could master the simple addition that would satisfy the editor on the other end of the phone, the story would hit the wire and recipients would hear the information they needed to know. When an unidentified man's body was brought to the city morgue, his skull crushed by the steel wheels of the El train, simple details superseded linguistic craft. When Nike opened its flagship Chicago store on Michigan Avenue, clarity was critical. When a Chicago Police Department violent crimes detective and commander was accused of using torture to elicit confessions, there was no room for error.

After stints at CNB, the *Chicago Tribune*, Tacoma's *News Tribune*, *The Oregonian*, and several weekly newspapers, I left journalism for academia. I loved the writing, but I struggled with the emotional turmoil of leaping from story to story without time to pause over the humanity of each loss, tragedy, crisis, or quandary. What the leaping taught me, though, was the necessity of simple math: 1 + 1 = 2. When an addend is missing or the sum does not equate, meaning is skewed or lost completely. Our brains are wired for linguistic structure, and our best, most efficient communication happens when that structure is honored. Yes, there is room for creativity beyond the basic structure, but the foundational elements of 1 + 1 = 2 must be accurately in place before we move on to higher levels.

Simple math demands a separation between essential and inessential rules of writing – a line too often muddied by well-meaning English teachers who allow their preferences to color the classroom. An essential rule is this: *A complete sentence must include a subject and a verb.* An inessential rule is this: *Sentences should not be too long.* I shuddered some years ago to hear a fellow professor commend a student paper as "wonderfully written, but with a few too many commas." A comment like that makes me want to visit a math class and compliment an assignment as "wonderfully computed, but with a few too many 2s." Both commentaries are equally ludicrous, and the former does not acknowledge the magnificent mathematical complexity of the language we use to share life with one another.

I, too, was educated by teachers whose variety of preferences was befuddling: short vs. long sentences, short vs. long paragraphs, short vs. long essays, contractions or no contractions, first person "I" or no first person "I," etc. In time, those conflicting voices can freeze your fingers over the keyboard, making it difficult to type anything at all without hearing a voice telling you that the choice you are making is incorrect. But if language is mathematical and your math is correct, those noisy voices from the past no longer get a vote. Once you understand the simple math of writing well, the only voice you should hear is your own, pressing you forward to communicate with speed, efficiency, and purpose.

We write now more than ever before in history, and as an English professor, I think it's magnificent: emails, texts, projects, papers, reviews, summaries, synopses, blogs, posts, reports, articles, lyrics, plans, essays, stories, books. For those of you born before about 1985, would you ever have imagined our newfound ease with the written word? And the stakes couldn't be higher. While family and friends may forgive us for silly typos, those we don't know well likely will not. We all shudder when we see an email from the colleague who writes in nine paragraphs what could be simply said in one. How do we learn to adhere to the simple math of language so those we are writing to focus on our content rather than getting sidetracked by linguistic trappings? How do we learn to write what we ourselves would like to read?

When you write, picture the tube: Who will receive your email, report, or essay? [Image: Esther Bubley [Public domain], via Wikimedia Commons]

For decades, City News Bureau was at the hub of a complex web of more than nine miles of pneumatic tubes spread throughout the city. When reporters called in to report a crime or a news event, rewrite men would type the story lightning-fast and then shoot it through the tubes to recipients all over the metropolitan area. Copy clerks monitored the tubes on the receiving end, watching for breaking news and deciding in a split-second whether to send a reporter out or report a story over the air. The CNB rewrite editors knew that if a story contained errors that sent other reporters to a wrong address or misrepresented a politician, the angry phone calls would start and their jobs could be lost. The price was high, and mistakes were few.

When you write, picture the tube: Who will receive your email, report, or essay? How will they respond when they twist open the capsule, and how can you ensure that your simple math is correct and your meaning is definitive and clear?

INTRODUCTION: MYTHS AND RULE CHANGES

1 + 1 = 2

Yes, the rules sometimes change, and yes, some of us were poorly taught, but the rules are not infinite, and they only change after decades of natural cultural shift. Once you know the basics, you will have the confidence to write in your own natural voice and then punctuate those words with accuracy and nuance. In an era when each of us is writing in a variety of mediums every day, the goal is to produce writing that is (1) clear, (2) concise, (3) accurate, and (4) appropriate. Don't let erroneous or obsolete mechanics prevent your readers from hearing your voice. The purpose of writing is to communicate content that is meaningful, memorable, and persuasive, which means that despite the time it takes to craft your mechanics well, the best-placed commas and periods are completely unseen.

The rules of basketball gave me confidence, and the space between the rules allowed me to be me. The same can be true when we write. [Image: Dan Carlson | Unsplash]

One reason I enjoyed playing basketball in my elementary and high school years was for the sheer simplicity of the sport: The rules were finite, consistent, and – for the most part – unchanging. Once the players accepted the boundaries of the rules, that was when finesse and creativity began: a sideways pass, a defensive screen, a sudden left hook. As point guard, I could dribble the ball down court with my right hand while my left hand was raised with a number, and my teammates would magically scurry across the court in the pattern we had prearranged. The rules gave me confidence, and the space between the rules allowed me to be me.

The same can be true when we write. Yes, American English is arguably one of the richest, most nuanced languages in the world. With roughly one million words and counting, the English language is complicated by its scaffolding of influences from a variety of other languages: Latin, Greek, French, Italian, German, Norman, Dutch, Celtic, Spanish, Arabic, Indian,

Hebrew, and Yiddish. Yes, there is a basic mathematical structure beneath, and yes, there are frequent deviations from the standard equations, but all is manageable once you begin to see the 1 + 1 = 2 that undergirds the complexities.

The rules of writing are manageable once you begin to see the 1 + 1 = 2 that undergirds the complexities. [Image: Julian Alexander | Unsplash]

HERE IS WHERE SOME OF THE CONUNDRUMS OF THE ENGLISH LANGUAGE LIE:

- **Idioms:** An *idiom* is a group of words whose combined meaning is entirely different from the meaning of the individual words. Typically the meaning arises from a metaphor, story, or event, but not always.
    - *He jumped the gun.*
      He moved too quickly.
    - *She felt sicker than a dog.*
      She felt very ill.

- *Yesterday it was raining cats and dogs.*
  Yesterday it rained very hard.
- *His personality rubs me the wrong way.*
  His personality irritates me.
- *That car costs an arm and a leg.*
  The car is very expensive.
- *Why does she feel the need to cut corners?*
  Why does she choose the easy way, skipping important components?
- *I think we should let sleeping dogs lie.*
  I think we should leave the situation as it is so we don't cause problems.
- *He missed the boat with that proposal today.*
  He missed his chance with the proposal today.
- *Everyone decided to jump on the bandwagon.*
  Everyone decided to join in.
- *She wouldn't be caught dead wearing that coat.*
  She finds the coat distasteful and would never wear it.

The English language is rarely static. Picture a river that is winding its way towards the ocean, slowing to a placid flow in the summer and fall and swelling to a bubbling rush in the winter and spring. A stick or leaf thrown into the river is tossed and pressed by the waters, occasionally trapped beneath a stone or tree root as it is pushed along toward the ocean. When a new idea or moment in history enters our linguistic timeline, it sends ripples through the culture in a forward-moving, continually shifting way.

Here is the linguistic line idioms often travel:

$$\text{Event} \rightarrow \text{Simile} \rightarrow \text{Metaphor} \rightarrow \text{Idiom}$$

For example, if I say I can be ready *at the drop of a hat*, you know that I will be ready instantly at your urging and won't cause you any delay. A non-English speaker would likely have little understanding of what *drop* or *hat* have to do with getting ready, but history buffs will know that the early 19th century was a time when men wore hats and those hats were sometimes used to start an event: When the signaler dropped his hat in a downward sweep, the race or fight began.

A simile is a figure of speech that includes the words *like* or *as*: *I will be as ready to go as a Wild West gunfighter waiting for the drop of a hat.* A metaphor is a figure of speech that closely mirrors the simile but does not include the words *like* or *as*; unlike an idiom, the meaning of a metaphor can typically be discerned by the context of the sentence: *I will be a Wild West gunfighter, ready to fight at the drop of a hat.* The complexity of the idiom is that it sheds all contexts and often we are left with a phrase that holds meaning for native speakers, but even we may not know the origins of that meaning. We may strive for clarity with the words we choose, but when the words gather together in English-typical idiomatic ways, is clarity truly possible?

- **Homonyms, Homophones, & Heteronyms:** English has many words that have multiple meanings and often are pronounced differently depending on the meaning intended, which can lead to further confusion as we strive to communicate well. Homonyms ("same meaning"), homophones ("same sound"), and heteronyms ("different meaning") are symptomatic of a language so heavily influenced by other languages and cultures.

  - *Homonyms* are words that are pronounced and spelled the same but have different meanings.

- The price seemed *fair* to me.
  He can't wait to go to the *fair*.

- I asked him to *lie* down.
  She said she would never *lie* to me.

- His left *foot* is bigger than his right.
  I am happy to *foot* the bill this time.

○ *Homophones* are words that are pronounced the same but have different meanings and sometimes-different spellings.

- The squirrel is in the tree over *there*.
  Why won't the children pick up *their* toys?
  I wonder when *they're* planning to come home.

- He ran *to* the bus.
  She would like to go to the movie, *too*.
  I ate *two* sandwiches yesterday.

○ *Heteronyms* are words that are spelled the same but have different pronunciations and different meanings.

- She wore a red *bow* in her hair.
  I was told to *bow* deeply after finishing my performance.
  He stood at the *bow* of the boat, watching for whales.

- The cat stared at the shiny *object* in the grass.
  I *object* to your angry tone.

As with idioms, the best approach for learning homonyms, homophones, and heteronyms is to continually ask clarifying questions when you are on the receiving end. When you are writing, always consider whether your audience will hear your meaning clearly. The onus is on the writer to always, always know his or her audience well long before pressing the "send" button.

- **Oxymorons:** An *oxymoron* is a phrase whose words have

contradictory meaning. While some oxymorons are ironic and intentional, many are not and can cause confusion. Most are so deeply embedded in our language that we don't even realize what they are.

- *an exact estimate*
  a precise amount
- *a crash landing*
  a tragic crash
- *a devout atheist*
  someone who is firm in his or her unbelief
- *old news*
  information that is no longer new
- *a minor miracle*
  a surprising and happy occurrence
- *loosely sealed*
  shut, but not too tightly
- *seriously funny*
  very funny
- *a small crowd*
  a gathering of people, although not too large
- *a working vacation*
  a trip where one plans to continue working
- *an unbiased opinion*
  an opinion that is not swayed by popular thought

As with all figures of speech, writers must be aware of their audience and whether unintended oxymorons could lead those readers astray. How old are your readers? What race, class, gender, religion, education, and culture?

- **Context:** A *higher-context culture* is relational and interpersonal, with assumed common contexts that make it possible for individuals to leave many things unspoken; higher-context cultures are more common in countries where there is low racial diversity. Individuals in a *lower-context culture*, on the other hand, tend to be explicit in their communication.

- ○ ***High-context cultures include***
  Afghan, African, Arabic, Brazilian, Chinese, Filipino. French Canadian, French, Greek, Hawaiian, Hungarian, Indian, Indonesian, Italian, Irish, Japanese, Korean, Latin American, Nepali, Pakistani, Persian, Portuguese, Russian, Slavic, Spanish, Thai, Turkish, Vietnamese.

- ○ ***Low-context cultures include*** *Australian, Dutch, English Canadian, English, Finnish, German, Israeli, New Zealander, Scandinavian, Swiss, American.*

Specific regions of the United States are considered higher context than others – the South, for example – but the United States overall is a lower-context culture; we are more individualistic, less dependent on shared experiences, and more likely to use words to explain ourselves thoroughly. The challenge, however, is we are a lower-context culture with a higher-context language. As we see in the examples above, American English is deeply embedded with idioms and mythologies that are culture- and history-dependent rather than word-dependent. We may use copious words to explain ourselves, but are the words we use conveying the meaning we intend?

- **Exceptions:** The rule exceptions in English are frequent and sometimes surprising with variations in pronunciation, spelling, and syntax. Most of these exceptions are symptoms of a language heavily influenced by a multicultural society, and many can be traced to the language of origin. It is not uncommon for languages to have irregularities; Russian and

Chinese are two languages known for their rule exceptions and complex syntax. While most native English speakers bemoan the rule exceptions, the tendency of American English to be culture-rich and metaphor-dependent is a far more unique and perplexing dynamic.

American English is deeply embedded with idioms and mythologies that are culture- and history-dependent rather than word-dependent. We may use copious words to explain ourselves, but are the words we use conveying the meaning we intend? [Image: Aaron Burden | Unsplash]

Sometimes the rules change, and sometimes the rules are not taught correctly in the first place. As we seek to differentiate between essential and inessential rules, be sure you discard the rules that should be forgotten.

HERE ARE 12 RULES TO FORGET:

1. **"Do not begin a sentence with a conjunction."**
   Elementary school teachers often tell students to avoid beginning a sentence with *and* or *but* because a young writer might write a fragment rather than a full sentence: *And the dog*. But feel free to start sentences with conjunctions. And do it as often as you like, as long as your purpose and your audience are well served.

2. **"Do not split an infinitive."**
   This rule likely refers to Latin, where an infinitive is a single word and therefore impossible to split: *to see* is *videre*, for example. But in English, where an infinitive is always to + verb, it is often necessary to split the infinitive in order to avoid awkwardness and confusion. *The university plans to more than double its enrollment in the next decade* would be a difficult sentence to reword without the *more than* sitting between the infinitive words *to* and *double*.

3. **"Do not end a sentence with a preposition."**
   In Latin grammar, the preposition must always precede the prepositional object with which it is linked. Although many students were taught this years ago, contemporary grammarians agree that – like the split infinitive – it is not necessary to force Latin rules onto English grammar, particularly when the model leaves standard sentences twisted and confused.
   Consider the following acceptable sentence-ending prepositions below:

   > **Examples**
   >
   > We wondered where the kitten had come from.
   > The child got into the bathtub once it was filled all the way up.
   > When I shouted his name, he looked over.

> *When she stepped off the escalator, she was careful to step down.*
> *He always prefers it when his children are near.*

4. **"Place commas and periods where you have a natural pause."**

   I frequently meet students who have been taught this rule, and I am always amazed by our loose definitions of *natural* and *pause*. I have days when I am fatigued and my pauses are frequent, and then I have other days when I am well caffeinated and I hardly pause at all. Would I skip commas on the latter days and use them copiously on the former? If you were taught this rule, please remove it from your brain. Commas and periods follow simple mathematical rules, as do all punctuation marks in the English language.

5. **"The serial comma is unnecessary."**

   The serial comma is the comma immediately preceding the conjunction in a list. In the example *We went to the store to buy apples, oranges, and bananas*, the comma just before the conjunction *and* is the serial comma. Also known as the *Oxford comma* in recognition of the Oxford University Press preference for the comma, the serial comma first came into discussion among grammarians in the late 1800s. Most current academic style guides mandate the use of the comma, including APA, MLA, and Turabian. The *Associated Press Stylebook*, used by journalists and public relations specialists nationwide, advises against its use unless absolutely necessary. In a 2017 U.S. court case, the absence of a serial comma led to ambiguity and allowed the court to interpret a rule more narrowly than might have been intended. If you plan to be a journalist, review the AP's current recommendations. If you don't plan to be a journalist, use the serial comma in every list you write.

6. **"Periods and commas go inside or outside quotation marks depending on the situation."**

While British English calls from commas and periods inside quotation marks in certain situations and outside quotation marks in others, the rule in the United States is simple: periods and commas always go inside quotation marks. Consider the following:

> **Examples**
>
> Her father explained that the mini orange is called a "kumquat," but the girl wasn't sure she wanted to try one.
>
> "We need to get the project done today," the woman said.

With the increasing popularity of machine typesetting in the late 19th century, typesetters determined that it was easier to nest the minor comma and period keys inside the heavier quotation mark keys rather than risk losing or displacing the thin slices of metal. American grammarians agreed to the change; British English users chose to hold onto King's English.

7. **"Use two spaces after periods and other terminal punctuation."**
   Typing two spaces after a period suggests to your readers that you are over 40 years old and have not paid attention to current practices. Typewriters in the 19th and 20th centuries used non-proportional fonts, which means each letter and character occupied the same width on the page. For reading ease, typists used two spaces after periods, question marks, exclamation points, colons, and semicolons. With the introduction of the computer era and an increasing variety of flexible fonts, double sentence spacing or "French spacing" became unnecessary. While the APA stylebook allows for one or two spaces after a period, all other American grammar and style guides have called for

just one space since the late 1990s. Unless you have a professor who insists on two spaces, use one.
8. **"Use 'an' before vowels and 'a' before consonants."**
Many of us were taught this article rule, but it is missing one critical word: *sound*. Here it is again: *Use "an" before vowel sounds and "a" before consonant sounds*. Consider these examples, which fit under the corrected rule but not under the former:

> **Examples**
>
> *He woke up an hour before his alarm.*
> *She earned an MBA last year.*
> *Did you earn an A on your exam?*
> *At least he gave an honest answer.*
> *She never intended to be a one-hit wonder.*

Speaking of articles, when the word "the" comes before a consonant sound, we pronounce it with the short *thuh* sound; when "the" comes before a vowel sound, we pronounce it *thee*: *thuh* house, *thee* university, *thuh* hamburger, *thee* opposite.

9. **"Always use active voice."**
While active voice is typically more engaging for readers, there can be instances where passive voice is more appropriate. When a writer uses active voice, the main subject of the sentence performs the action of the main verb. Consider the following examples of active voice:

> **Examples**
>
> *The boy rode his bicycle.*

> *The girl sprinted past the skate park.*
> *Everyone shouted at once.*

When a writer uses passive voice, the subject of the sentence receives the action of the verb or the agent of the action is omitted entirely. A sentence in passive voice often requires more words and can seem distanced or flat. But in scientific and technical writing, passive voice is sometimes preferred because it sounds more objective. Consider the following examples of passive voice:

> **Examples**
>
> *The test tube samples were isolated on Friday and tested again on Monday.*
> *The carburetor was replaced twice in one year.*
> *Sixteen new items were listed on Craig's List yesterday.*

Be aware of the difference between active and passive voice, and choose the mode that best fits your audience and purpose.

10. **"Do not use first-person pronouns."**
    While the first-person pronouns "I", "we", and "us" are sometimes inappropriate in writing that is intended to be objective and impersonal, the dictate that first-person pronouns should never be used is grossly misleading. Purpose and audience are always the best determinants in writing, and too often writers who avoid the first-person "I" produce writing that is cumbersome and unclear. Unless you have a professor, boss, or situation that overtly forbids the use of first person, use "I" freely to bring clarity and distinction to your writing.

11. **"Do not use slang."**
    A better rule is to, instead, focus on what you *should* be

doing: paying keen attention to your purpose and audience. Any word choices you make – from slang to King's English – will directly affect how your audience perceives you and your ideas. While slang phrases like *three sheets to the wind, emo,* and *easy-peasy* would be inappropriate in an academic essay or an email to your board of directors, such language can sometimes bolster your credibility with an audience that otherwise might be distrustful.

Like slang, overly formal language can make you sound stilted or insincere. "Heretofore" or "thereafter", for example, could be off-putting in an email to a coworker or appear unnatural in an academic essay when you don't normally speak that way. As always, consider the predilections of your audience and the finer nuances of your purpose, and make your decisions regarding word choice accordingly.

12. **"Do not use contractions."**
As with slang, your use of contractions depends on your audience. In academic writing, an overuse of contractions can sound informal, rushed, and even uneducated. In many emails, the avoidance of contractions, on the other hand, can make one sound proud or even egotistic. If you were taught to eliminate all contractions from your writing, erase that rule from your repertoire. Instead focus your attention on the purpose of your work and the audience to whom you are writing, and decide whether contractions would be inclusive or off-putting for those you intend to reach.

PART I.

THE SENTENCE EQUATION

Most of us are aware that we begin to learn math by adding together the simplest components: 1 apple + 1 apple = 2 apples. When children struggle to grasp higher mathematical constructs, we remind them of the importance of mastering their math facts. But somehow in our frustrated assumption that good writing is an arbitrary, ill-defined mystery, we have forgotten one important truth: We acquire language in much the same way that we learn math. And when we are struggling to write effectively at levels higher than what our kindergarten teacher once required, there is no shame in revisiting the simple linguistic equations that lead to effective communication. Equation #1: Just as 1 +1 = 2, a subject + a verb = a sentence.

CHAPTER 1.

MAIN VERBS

The verb is the engine of the sentence. [Image: Alternate Skate | Unsplash]

DEFINITION TO REMEMBER:

- **Verb = Action**

Every sentence must have two components in order to be a sentence: a subject and a verb. The verb is the engine of the sentence. It either provides the **action** that gives the sentence life or functions as the **link** between the subject and its modifier.

When you look for the main verb in a sentence, look first for a linking verb: am, is, are, was, were, being, been, etc. Common linking verbs include variations of *to be, to become,* and *to seem,* among others.

If you see a linking verb, it will nearly always be the main verb of your sentence: *The pen is blue. The movie was sad.* If you don't see a linking verb, look for the word that defines the action in your sentence: *I threw the pen across the room. The dog barked.*

RULES TO REMEMBER:

1. If you see a linking verb, it will nearly always be your main verb. If a linking verb is part of an introductory or concluding phrase, it cannot be the main verb; otherwise, it will be the main verb.

    ◦ *That pillow is soft.*

    ◦ *Her brother seems angry.*

    ◦ *The front door will be open tomorrow afternoon.*

2. A gerund (-ing verb) must have a helper verb in order to be your main verb.

    ◦ *He had been walking for more than an hour before arriving.* Had been walking is the main verb; *arriving* has no helper verb and cannot be the main verb.

> **"Good writing expresses what you mean to say, but great writing can ignite the imagination, give power to a cause, unite communities, and change the world for the better. Don't just be a good writer. Be a great one."** *Jennifer Hebbeler, Accounting Specialist*

- *The kindergartner was sitting alone at the beginning of class, waiting for her friend.*
  Was sitting is the main verb; *waiting* has no helper verb and cannot be the main verb.

3. An infinitive (to + verb) can never be your main verb.

    - *My teenager waited nine months to get her driver's license.*
      Waited is the main verb; *to get* is an infinitive and cannot be the main verb.

    - *He is almost ready to jump into the deep end of the swimming pool.*
      Is is the main verb; *to jump* is an infinitive and cannot be the main verb.

4. Your main verb will not be part of an introductory or concluding phrase.

    - *Even though the bus arrived late, she still made it to work on time.*
      Made is the main verb; *arrived* is part of an introductory phrase and cannot be the main verb.

    - *While the mother duck ushered her ducklings across the busy road, the cars waited patiently.*
      Waited is the main verb; *ushered* is part of an introductory phrase and cannot be the main verb.

5. Watch for the compound verb, which occurs when a single main subject completes two or more actions in a single sentence.

    - <u>I ran</u> to my car and <u>grabbed</u> my umbrella. (I + ran, grabbed)
    - <u>Jeff</u> never <u>sleeps</u> or <u>eats</u> well in another city. (Jeff + sleeps, eats)
    - Once he woke from his nap, the <u>baby chattered</u> and <u>clapped</u>

joyfully for most of the afternoon. (baby + chattered, clapped)

6. Always look for the verb first. Once you locate your main verb, the other components of the sentence will be easier to find.

    - *Jordan has been dieting this summer, trying to lose a few pounds.*
    Has been is the main verb.
    - *Arthur baked four batches of lemon muffins this morning.*
    Baked is the main verb.
    - *I was terribly thirsty after our long hike through the mountains.*
    Was is the main verb.

7. In colloquial speech or written dialogue, the verb can sometimes be implied. Do not rely on an implied verb in formal or academic writing.

    - "Who will be with you on the bus?"
    "Thomas.
    Will be is the implied verb, as in *Thomas will be with me on the bus.*

COMMON ERRORS:

- **Forgetting the verb.**

    - *Elizabeth was hoping to meet us, but not yet. After the dance.* What action occurs *after the dance*? This fragment is missing both a subject and a verb. Either join the fragment with another sentence, or add the necessary components: *She will meet us after the dance.*

- **Mismatching the subject and verb.**

- *His girls, who finally got a hamster from the store to keep as a pet, convinces everyone that the hamster needs a second hamster for company.*
  His girls is plural, which means *convince* must be a plural verb: girls + convince.

- **Varying the verb tense.**

  - *Every Sunday, the boy studied his Spanish vocabulary, and every Saturday, he practices verb conjugation.*
    Studied and *practices* should either both be in present tense (*studies and practices*) or both be in past tense (*studied and practiced*).

EXERCISES:

Exercise 1.1

Identify the main verb in the following sentences.

1. My grandmother rides her scooter to the market across town.
2. His sister drinks her lattes with coconut milk and two extra shots of espresso.
3. He hopes to earn a degree in human resources one day.
4. The plant at the end of the hallway looks thirsty.
5. The lightning flashed suddenly and loudly.
6. I have never ridden in a boat this large.
7. Josephine likes her house cool in the winter and warm in the summer.
8. That cat must have nine lives.
9. Enjoy your trip.
10. Are the eggs finished yet?

Exercise 1.2

Identify the main verb in the following sentences.

1. Once I arrive, we will discuss the details.
2. After yesterday's baseball game, his baseball paints were ripped in three places.
3. What time is the meeting?
4. You should talk to her later, when you both have time to sit and think things through.
5. She has always dreamed of living in the country, where the crickets sing and the stars are bright.
6. When he plays the guitar, his inhibitions disappear.
7. Sixteen horses are corralled in the far pasture, waiting to be brought into the barn.
8. The subway arrives every 20 minutes on the red line.
9. My professor warned me about that textbook.
10. Her exam passed with highest honors, much to her surprise.

Exercise 1.3

Identify and correct the verb errors in the following paragraph.

Sonia started her first waitressing job on Thursday. On Thursday and Friday, she shadows another waitress, following her from table to table. On Saturday morning, the restaurant manager asks if she wanted to serve her first table alone. Sonia said yes, but she was so nervous that her hands shooked as she walked to the table. Two teenage girls sat sullenly at the table, hardly acknowledging Sonia as they order milkshakes and nachos. Sonia wrote the order on her notepad and thanks the girls. When she submitted the order, the cook reminded her to clips the order to the left of the heat lamps. Sonia scooped chocolate ice cream into the metal milkshake cups and turns the blender on high. When the milkshakes are blended, she squirted swirls of whipped cream on the top of each shake. The girls grinned when Sonia brought their order to the table, and Sonia's nervousness finally begins to fade. Two more tables fill, and Sonia scurried to help.

ANSWER KEY:

Answer Key Exercise 1.1

1. My grandmother <u>rides</u> her scooter to the market across town.
2. His sister <u>drinks</u> her lattes with coconut milk and two extra shots of espresso.
3. He <u>hopes</u> to earn a degree in human resources one day.
4. The plant at the end of the hallway <u>looks</u> thirsty.
5. The lightning <u>flashed</u> suddenly and loudly.
6. I <u>have</u> never ridden in a boat this large.
7. Josephine <u>likes</u> her house cool in the winter and warm in the summer.
8. That cat <u>must</u> have nine lives.
9. <u>Enjoy</u> your trip.
10. <u>Are</u> the eggs finished yet?

Answer Key Exercise 1.2

1. Once I arrive, we <u>will</u> discuss the details.
2. After yesterday's baseball game, his baseball paints <u>were</u> ripped in three places.
3. What time <u>is</u> the meeting?
4. You <u>should</u> talk to her later, when you both have time to sit and think things through.

5. She <u>has</u> always dreamed of living in the country, where the crickets sing and the stars are bright.
6. When he plays the guitar, his inhibitions <u>disappear</u>.
7. Sixteen horses <u>are</u> corralled in the far pasture, waiting to be brought into the barn.
8. The subway <u>arrives</u> every 20 minutes on the red line.
9. My professor <u>warned</u> me about that textbook.
10. Her exam <u>passed</u> with highest honors, much to her surprise.

Answer Key Exercise 1.3

Sonia started her first waitressing job on Thursday. On Thursday and Friday, she <u>shadowed</u> another waitress, following her from table to table. On Saturday morning, the restaurant manager <u>asked</u> if she wanted to serve her first table alone. Sonia said yes, but she was so nervous that her hands <u>shook</u> as she walked to the table. Two teenage girls sat sullenly at the table, hardly acknowledging Sonia as they <u>ordered</u> milkshakes and nachos. Sonia wrote the order on her notepad and <u>thanked</u> the girls. When she submitted the order, the cook reminded her to <u>clip</u> the order to the left of the heat lamps. Sonia scooped chocolate ice cream into the metal milkshake cups and <u>turned</u> the blender on high. When the milkshakes <u>were</u> blended, she squirted swirls of whipped cream on the top of each shake. The girls grinned when Sonia brought their order to the table, and Sonia's nervousness finally <u>began</u> to fade. Two more tables <u>filled</u>, and Sonia scurried to help.

CHAPTER 2.

MAIN SUBJECTS

Always find the verb first. Once you do, ask yourself, "Who or what is doing the action?"
[Image: Matthew Henry | Unsplash]

DEFINITION TO REMEMBER:

- **Subject = Who/what is doing the action**

Always find the verb first. Once you do, ask yourself, "Who or what is doing the action?" Picture the action in your mind. Is the answer you have come up with logical? Are the action you have named and the subject you have identified the chief intent of the sentence?

If you have been taught to think of a subject as a person, place, or thing, be careful. A noun is a person, place, or thing, but the main subject of a sentence can be more: a verb phrase, an adjectival phrase, or even an implied entity.

If your main verb is a linking verb, the "Who or what is doing the action?" may need a little finessing. For example, consider this sentence: *The hotel carpet is colorful.* If you have named *is* as your main verb, ask yourself, "Who or what *is?*" Your answer should be *carpet*.

A helpful trick: To locate the main subject and main verb, begin by eliminating the factors that you know cannot contain the main subject or main verb. Those include the following:

> "As a long-time manager of multiple departments, a critical skill I look for in hiring for management and professional positions is the ability to communicate well in writing. The ability to communicate well in emails, reports, and in other documents is a requirement for advancing in one's career." *Wes Friesen, Manager*

- **Prepositional phrases:** a 3- to 4-word phrase that begins with a preposition and ends with a noun, such as *on the floor, after the party, over the bridge,* etc.
- **Articles**: *the, a, an*
- **Infinitive verbs:** to + verb, such as *to run, to sit, to eat, to sleep*

- **Gerund verbs without helper verbs:** -ing verb, such as *running, sitting, eating, sleeping*
- **Introductory phrases:** *before the long drive, after I called him, on Monday*
- **Concluding phrases:** *before the long drive, after I called him, on Monday* (such phrases can go before or after the main sentence, depending on what you choose to emphasize).

Watch the following reduce from a lengthy sentence to simple math:

[~~After class today~~], the **woman** [~~with the brown sunglasses~~] **ran** [~~across the street~~] [~~to buy a latte~~] [~~before getting into her car~~].

After class today is a prepositional phrase and an introductory phrase; *the* is an article; *with the brown sunglasses* is a prepositional phrase; *across the street* is a prepositional phrase; *to buy a latte* is an infinitive verb; and *before getting into her car* is a prepositional phrase, a gerund verb, and a concluding phrase.

Do you see how the simple math emerges? As you learn to cross out the extraneous factors where a main subject and main verb cannot hide, you will begin to see the subject and verb emerge in every sentence.

Look online for lists of hundreds of prepositions. Here are a few:

about	down	past
above	for	since
across	from	to
after	in	toward
around	into	under
before	of	until
behind	off	up
below	on	with
beyond	onto	within
by	over	without

RULES TO REMEMBER:

1. If you are able, reduce the main subject and main verb to a single word each. Remember that the goal of Chapters 1 and 2 is to learn to identify the two key factors of the sentence equation: Just as 1 +1 = 2, a subject + a verb = a sentence. Once you are able to quickly spot the key factors of a sentence, run-ons and sentence fragments will no longer be an issue.

   - *The brown-haired <u>woman</u> with the red shirt <u>ran</u> past me first.* (woman + ran)
   - *The giant <u>leaves</u> of the palm tree <u>were</u> tinged with brown.* (leaves + were)
   - *The heavyset <u>waiter</u> <u>forgot</u> to take my order.* (waiter + forgot)

2. While there may be other subjects and nouns in your

sentence, remember that you are looking for the main subject. Slow down when you ask yourself "Who or what did the action?" and be sure you named the correct subject as your main subject.

- *After a long day of preparing depositions, the <u>attorney</u> <u>settled</u> into his art studio with his paintbrushes, a fresh canvas, and a Chopin prelude.* (attorney + settled)
- *The <u>cat</u> <u>ran</u> across the yard with his eyes wide with panic and his tale bushed out like a squirrel's.* (cat + ran)
- *Once his grandmother arrives, <u>Mark</u> <u>will</u> show her the china in the hall cabinet.* (Mark + will)

3. Watch for the compound main subject, which means you have more than one subject associated with the same main verb.

    - *The <u>mangoes</u> and the <u>papayas</u> <u>were</u> all bruised at the bottom of the grocery bag.* (mangoes, papayas + were) *<u>Richard</u> and <u>Stephanie</u> both <u>decided</u> to skip the concert tonight.* (Richard, Stephanie + decided)
    - *When he moved to his new apartment, his <u>friends</u> and his <u>family</u> <u>complained</u> about the number of heavy boxes of books that needed to be carried.* (friends, family + complained)

4. In colloquial speech or written dialogue, the subject can sometimes be implied. Do not rely on an implied subject in formal or academic writing.

    - *Wait!*
      You is the implied subject.
    - *When?*
      You is the implied subject here as well, as in *Do you know when?*

COMMON ERRORS:

- **Forgetting the main subject.**

  - *The two-year-old girl spun gleefully in circles across the green lawn. Skirt swirling, spinning and spinning.*
    Spinning is an effective compound main verb, but it is missing a subject. This sentence can be corrected by joining the fragment with the sentence just prior or by adding the missing subject: *Skirt swirling, she kept spinning and spinning.*

- **Mismatching the subject and verb.**

  - *The red-breasted robin, awake early in March and ready to announce the blooming crocuses, sing a beautiful melody as the sun begins to rise.*
    Robin is singular, which means the main verb must be singular as well: robin + sings.

- **Mistaking a prepositional phrase for the subject.**

  - *The pages of the book got wet in the rainstorm yesterday.*
    Of the book is a prepositional phrase, which will never contain your main subject. The main subject and main verb are as follows: pages + got. Take note that erroneous verbs often occur when a writer inadvertently assumes a noun in a prepositional phrase is the main subject.

EXERCISES:

Exercise 2.1

Identify the main subject in the following sentences.

1. The pitcher threw a fastball.
2. Jonah jumped over his brother.

3. The president of the company always arrives at the office before anyone else.
4. Under his coat, he wore a bright red sweater.
5. The lettuce in the salad drawer looks old to me.
6. I love a good hamburger.
7. The couple danced three waltzes last night.
8. My great grandmother always sewed all of her sons' clothes herself.
9. Her coworkers decided to throw her a surprise party.
10. He loves that kind of music, even with the odd backbeat.

Exercise 2.2

Identify the main subject in the following sentences.

1. Every election season, she keeps the news on every minute that she's awake.
2. When you wake up, you should raise the shades first thing to enjoy the mountain view.
3. Are we going to the movie together or separately?
4. He never schedules enough time to get all of his work done.
5. I put cherries in the red bowl on the counter.
6. When her dad was in high school, he learned to type on a manual typewriter.
7. The new veterinarian specializes in caring for large animals.
8. Their anniversary was yesterday.
9. That new dog doesn't realize that our yard is not part of his property.
10. When the police officer pulled her over, the woman explained that she had not seen the new speed limit sign.

Exercise 2.3

Identify and correct the subject and verb errors in the following paragraph.

When Lincoln started his new job at the physician's office, he weren't sure what he would be doing. On the first day, he follows Linda around to see what she did. He enjoys sitting at the front desk to greet patients and answer the phones. Gave him a tour of the office complex. Lincoln was learned how to log onto the computers in each exam room. After lunch, Lincoln was surprise to learn that much of Linda's time is spent talking to insurance companies. Linda gives Lincoln a link to a master list of insurance codes. Joked that he would rather just greet and care for patients. Linda agrees. After eight hours of shadowing Linda, was ready for his first day of work on his own.

ANSWER KEY:

Answer Key Exercise 2.1

1. The <u>pitcher</u> threw a fastball.
2. <u>Jonah</u> jumped over his brother.
3. The <u>president</u> of the company always arrives at the office before anyone else.
4. Under his coat, <u>he</u> wore a bright red sweater.
5. The <u>lettuce</u> in the salad drawer looks old to me.
6. <u>I</u> love a good hamburger.
7. The <u>couple</u> danced three waltzes last night.
8. My great <u>grandmother</u> always sewed all of her sons' clothes herself.
9. Her <u>coworkers</u> decided to throw her a surprise party.
10. <u>He</u> loves that kind of music, even with the odd backbeat.

Answer Key Exercise 2.2

1. Every election season, <u>she</u> keeps the news on every minute that she's awake.
2. When you wake up, <u>you</u> should raise the shades first thing to enjoy the mountain view.
3. Are <u>we</u> going to the movie together or separately?
4. <u>He</u> never schedules enough time to get all of his work done.
5. <u>I</u> put cherries in the red bowl on the counter.
6. When her dad was in high school, <u>he</u> learned to type on a manual typewriter.
7. The new <u>veterinarian</u> specializes in caring for large animals.
8. Their <u>anniversary</u> was yesterday.
9. That new <u>dog</u> doesn't realize that our yard is not part of his property.
10. When the police officer pulled her over, the <u>woman</u> explained that she had not seen the new speed limit sign.

Answer Key Exercise 2.3

When Lincoln started his new job at the physician's office, he <u>wasn't</u> sure what he would be doing. On the first day, he <u>followed</u> Linda around to see what she did. He <u>enjoyed</u> sitting at the front desk to greet patients and answer the phones. <u>Linda</u> gave him a tour of the office complex. Lincoln <u>learned</u> how to log onto the computers in each exam room. After lunch, Lincoln was <u>surprised</u> to learn that much of Linda's time is spent talking to insurance companies. Linda <u>gave</u> Lincoln a link to a master list of insurance codes. <u>Lincoln</u> joked that he would rather just greet and care for patients. Linda <u>agreed</u>. After eight hours of shadowing Linda, <u>Lincoln</u> was ready for his first day of work on his own.

CHAPTER 3.

TERMINAL PUNCTUATION MARKS

Terminal punctuation is used at the end of a sentence or question. Terminal = at the end. [Image: Anthony Indraus | Unsplash]

DEFINITIONS TO REMEMBER:

- **Periods:** Use only after a *subject + verb*.
  If you have been taught to add a period when your words seem conclusive or when you intend a longer pause, remember that we are learning to watch for the simple math. Just as a math teacher would not instruct you to add a "3"

when it feels right, do not rely on subjective feelings for the structure of language either. Instead watch for the math: *subject + verb = sentence*.

- **Question Marks:** Use only after a question, and often with the components reversed to *verb + subject*.
  Whether you have a direct question or a rhetorical question, use a question mark in place of a period. If you have an indirect question that is actually part of a statement, the question mark is not necessary: *She asked me whether I like pasta.* Just as with a period, watch for the key factors of subject + verb, although note that the two are often reversed to form a new equation: *verb + subject = question*.

- **Exclamation Points:** Use sparingly!
  The exclamation point is used to show emphasis. Overuse of the exclamation point typically means your language is weak, and you are working hard to ensure that your readers recognize the emotions you want to convey. Poor writing relies on the exclamation point; good writing relies on strong verbs and nuanced punctuation, making the exclamation point unnecessary. As with the period and the question mark, the same two key components are necessary: *subject + verb = exclamation*.

RULES TO REMEMBER:

1. For any of the three terminal punctuation marks – period, question mark, or exclamation point – you must have a *subject + verb*.

    - *She likes raspberry smoothies.* (she + likes)
    - *Where are the raspberries?* (are + raspberries)
    - *She drank it quickly!* (she + drank)

2. Both a direct and a rhetorical question must end with a punctuation mark.

- *What time is the graduation party?* (is + party)
- *How should I know?* (should + I)
  A rhetorical question is a question that does not need an answer. If, for example, a friend asks you whether you intend to join him for lunch, you might answer, "Does the sun rise in the east?" not because you are encouraging a discussion of the earth's rotation but because you want to emphasize that of course you intend to be there.

3. Exclamation points should not be used in formal or academic writing, and should be used only sparingly in casual writing. Instead of relying on the exclamation point for emphasis, use strong verbs, lively adjectives, and creative nouns. In most cases, reserve exclamation points for direct dialogue or emails/texts to people you know well.

   - *"Jump!" Anthony shouted to his friend on the diving board.*
   - *"Oh!" Louisa said with surprise. "What time were we supposed to arrive?"*

COMMON ERRORS:

- **Forgetting the subject.**

  - *Slammed the door in frustration.*
    Slammed is the verb, but we are missing a subject. Revision: *Joseph slammed the door in frustration.* (Joseph + slammed)

- **Forgetting the verb.**

  - *Children leaping and giggling in the giant ball pit.*

> "Writing in the workplace is about helping others make the connections between the everyday ordinary and the wonderful possibilities yet to be discovered."
> Paul Jones, Lead Pastor of Journey of Hope Community Church

Children is the subject, but we are missing a verb. Revision: *Children were leaping and giggling in the giant ball pit.* (children + were)

- **Forgetting the question mark.**

  ◦ *Why does he always have to behave that way.*
  Even though it is likely a rhetorical question, we still need a question mark: *Why does he always have to behave that way?* (does + he)

- **Overusing the exclamation point.**

  ◦ *The book was amazing!*

  ◦ *The author is brilliant!*

  ◦ *I look forward to exploring this topic further!*
  If you include exclamation points in formal or academic writing, don't be surprised if you lose a client or watch your final grade slide a few points. Exclamation points suggest that you are not confident about the strength of your words or ideas; if you want to write with conviction and authority, save the exclamation point for your texts to family and friends.

EXERCISES:

Exercise 3.1

Finish the following with a period, question mark, or exclamation point.

1. Why does your car always smell funny on Tuesdays
2. Olivia ran 16 miles yesterday in preparation for Saturday's race
3. That movie looks excellent

4. Does it matter whether I wear blue or yellow tomorrow afternoon
5. Forty-five years is a long time for two people to love one another so well
6. I wonder why his hair has flecks of paint in it today
7. Were you ever required to take a typing course in school
8. He will arrive in two hours
9. "Ouch"
10. Left-turns are difficult on this road

Exercise 3.2

Correct the following sentence fragments.

1. An answer to prayer.
2. Chugging along slowly down the highway.
3. Watering his lawn on a hot July day.
4. Just in case.
5. In her most professional attire.
6. Exhausted by a long day of assessment.
7. To the left of the stapler and to the right of the printer.
8. Trembling beneath three layers of blankets.
9. Uneasy about the day ahead.
10. Teenagers ready for summer.

Exercise 3.3

Correct the following run-on sentences.

1. I sliced the lemons with the new blade I sliced the corner of my index finger, too.
2. He slept all day yesterday, I wonder how well he will sleep tonight.
3. I know the bookshelves are dusty I can't think about it until after I meet this next deadline, though.
4. The kids rarely wanted to eat the same foods as their parents they preferred mostly white foods with a smattering of ketchup now and then.
5. Lucy decided that spring is her favorite season she loves to spot the new buds on the pear tree before anyone else in the family.
6. Last year, he had only one week of vacation time this year, he hopes to earn more.
7. Yesterday was a good day I finished my homework, cleaned my room, and jogged two miles.
8. She hopes to get her license on her 16th birthday her friends are excited to ride to school with her.
9. They decided to watch a movie last night it gave them nightmares.
10. We planted sunflowers in May they grew taller than the roof.

ANSWER KEY:

Answer Key Exercise 3.1

1. Why does your car always smell funny on Tuesdays?
2. Olivia ran 16 miles yesterday in preparation for Saturday's race.
3. That movie looks excellent.
4. Does it matter whether I wear blue or yellow tomorrow afternoon?
5. Forty-five years is a long time for two people to love one another so well.
6. I wonder why his hair has flecks of paint in it today.

7. Were you ever required to take a typing course in school?
8. He will arrive in two hours.
9. "Ouch!"
10. Left-turns are difficult on this road.

Answer Key Exercise 3.2

A variety of answers will work, as long as each sentence includes a subject and a verb.

1. <u>She was</u> an answer to prayer.
2. <u>Their motorhome was</u> chugging along slowly down the highway.
3. <u>He was</u> watering his lawn on a hot July day.
4. <u>I will call her</u> just in case.
5. <u>She arrived</u> in her most professional attire.
6. <u>He was</u> exhausted by a long day of assessment.
7. <u>The paper is</u> to the left of the stapler and to the right of the printer.
8. <u>The feverish child lay</u> trembling beneath three layers of blankets.
9. <u>I am</u> uneasy about the day ahead.
10. <u>They were just</u> teenagers ready for summer.

Answer Key Exercise 3.3

1. I sliced the lemons with the new blade. I sliced the corner of my index finger, too.
2. He slept all day yesterday. I wonder how well he will sleep tonight.

3. I know the bookshelves are dusty. I can't think about it until after I meet this next deadline, though.
4. The kids rarely wanted to eat the same foods as their parents. They preferred mostly white foods with a smattering of ketchup now and then.
5. Lucy decided that spring is her favorite season. She loves to spot the new buds on the pear tree before anyone else in the family.
6. Last year, he had only one week of vacation time. This year, he hopes to earn more.
7. Yesterday was a good day. I finished my homework, cleaned my room, and jogged two miles.
8. She hopes to get her license on her 16th birthday. Her friends are excited to ride to school with her.
9. They decided to watch a movie last night. It gave them nightmares.
10. We planted sunflowers in May. They grew taller than the roof.

CHAPTER 4.

MID-SENTENCE PUNCTUATION MARKS

Just as terminal punctuation comes at the end of a sentence, mid-sentence punctuation is used somewhere in the middle. Examples include the comma, semicolon, colon, dash, hyphen, apostrophe, and quotation marks. [Image: Hieu Vu Minh | Unsplash]

DEFINITIONS TO REMEMBER:

- **Comma:** Use (1) in a list of three or more; (2) with compound adjectives; (3) before a FANBOYS conjunction to join two sentences; (4) with interrupters; (5) with direct quotations; and (6) when you really, really want to ensure clarity for your readers.

- **Semicolon:** Use (1) in place of a period or (2) in a complex list.
- **Colon:** Use (1) to introduce, (2) to denote time, or (3) in a mathematical equation.
- **Dash:** Use (1) to introduce or (2) with interrupters.
- **Hyphen:** Use to join words that have combined meaning.
- **Apostrophe:** Use (1) to show possession or (2) to show something is missing.
- **Quotation Marks:** Use standard quotation marks (1) with direct quotes or (2) with titles of smaller works, such as a single song, a poem, or a journal article. Use single quotes only when you have a quote within a quote.
- **Ellipses:** Use (1) to show missing material or (2) to suggest suspense in non-professional writing.
- **Bracket:** Use (1) to clarify meaning or (2) for a parenthetical within a parenthetical.
- **Slash:** Use (1) to indicate a line break in poetry or (2) to serve as shorthand for *or* or *and*.

RULES TO REMEMBER:

1. The **comma** should not be used "when you feel the need to pause" or "sprinkled sparingly," as some have been erroneously taught. Just as terminal punctuation fits a simple mathematical equation, so, too, does the comma. The rules are simple, and there are only six. Practice the ones that don't already seem familiar, and set aside the guess-work:

    ◦ **In a List:** Between items in a series of three or more.

- *My husband loves to cook curry, egg, beef, and vegetarian main dishes.*
- *The store sells adult and teen sizes.*

The Oxford or serial comma is the comma before *and* in the first example above. While some formatting styles still declare its use optional, court cases have reached questionable conclusions because of that missing comma. The verdict: Use it, always. It is not worth leaving your readers wondering when the items of a list can be easily clarified with the habitual use of a serial comma. In the example above, wouldn't many readers pause to wonder about the complexity of a "beef and vegetarian main dish" if the serial comma were omitted? Never give your readers reason to wonder about the clarity of your ideas.In addition, do not use a comma in a list of two, even if you are concerned about clarity. A comma in a list of two will likely lead your reader to re-read, wondering if an item is missing. Readers should never have to read your work again because they did not understand your meaning the first time.

> "Communicating clearly and efficiently is crucial to accomplishing ordinary tasks, and intelligent written communication supports my reputation as a professional. I rely on my reputation to establish a network that broadens my career horizons."
> *Elizabeth Sobol, Chemical Buyer*

- **After Adjectives:** To separate two or more coordinate

adjectives (descriptive words that are of equal importance) that describe a noun.

- *The old, beloved Honda was ready for the highway.*
- *My neighbor is a frustrated, angry young woman.*
  The key to deciding if you have coordinate adjectives is to ask two questions: (1) Does the sentence make sense if the adjectives are written in reverse order? (2) Does the sentence make sense if the adjectives are written with *and* between them? If the answer is yes, you have coordinate adjectives and you need to separate them with a comma.

○ **To Connect Sentences:** Before any of the seven FANBOYS coordinating conjunctions: for, and, nor, but, or, yet, so.

- *I read the entire article, but I could not understand its purpose.*
- *I drove my daughter to work yesterday, and then I drove to the grocery store.*

○ **With Interrupters:** To separate phrases of additional information that can occur in the beginning, middle, or end of a sentence.

- Beginning: *In Minneapolis, my mother was a dentist.*
  Middle: *My mother, a dentist, was not pleased to hear that I had stopped brushing my teeth.*
  End: *My mother studied dentistry for four years, which means she lived in Boston before settling in Minneapolis.*

○ **With Direct Quotations:** To shift from your original words to a quote.

- William Faulkner once said, "Always dream and shoot

higher than you know you can do. Do not bother just to be better than your contemporaries or predecessors. Try to be better than yourself."

- **When Necessary:** When meaning is more clear with a comma than without.

2. The **semicolon** has only two uses: (1) in place of a period and (2) in a complex list.

    - *The author argues vehemently in favor of the new environmental impact study; her ideas echo those of several worthy contemporaries.*

    - *The horses are standing at the back gate, waiting to be brought in for the night; however, I would rather wait until the sun goes down to bring them in.*

    - *My cousin is planning to bring her mother, a physics professor; her brother, a nuclear scientist; and her husband, an accomplished chef.*

    - *This summer, we plan to visit Detroit, Michigan; Flagstaff, Arizona; Hartford, Connecticut; and Juneau, Alaska.*

3. The **colon** is primarily used to introduce, although it is also used when we write time (8:10 a.m.) or occasionally in mathematical equations. When it is used to introduce, a colon must always be preceded by a complete sentence.

    - *The casserole my grandchildren love has four main ingredients: cooked spaghetti, fresh tomato sauce, ricotta cheese, and mozzarella cheese.*

    - *The author's argument slips somewhat on p. 129: Here he is debating the merits of a 1990s survey, and his discussion does not directly relate to his overall claim.*
    Note in the above example that when the colon is

followed by a complete sentence, the first word of the sentence should be capitalized.

4. The **dash** is used for only two purposes: (1) to introduce (in place of a colon) or to separate an interrupter (in place of commas or parentheses). To form a dash, type two hyphens. Some style guides allow a space before and after the dash, and some do not. While the dash is considered a less formal punctuation mark, it can be used in professional and academic writing. Be careful of overusing the dash, as it will bring your readers to a fuller pause than merely a comma.

   - *When you are ready to go, don't forget the most important item – her gift.*
   - *Their new puppy was beautiful – wide-eyed, long-haired, pink-tongued – and made me wonder whether our aging dog would like a new friend one day.*

   Note that the interrupter in the second example could be surrounded by any of three punctuation marks: commas, dashes, or parentheses. **Commas** will keep your readers moving steadily forward, **dashes** will encourage your reader to pause over the interrupter, and **parentheses** will often allow your readers to skip over the interrupter all together. Consider the differences:

   - With commas: *Their new puppy was beautiful, wide-eyed, long-haired, pink-tongued, and made me wonder whether our aging dog would like a new friend one day.*
   - With dashes: *Their new puppy was beautiful – wide-eyed, long-haired, pink-tongued – and made me wonder whether our aging dog would like a new friend one day.*
   - With parentheses: *Their new puppy was beautiful (wide-eyed, long-haired, pink-tongued) and made me wonder whether our aging dog would like a new friend one day.*

5. The **hyphen** is used to join words that function as a single unit of meaning, and it is typically aid your reader in understanding more clearly what you intend. Hyphens became increasingly more popular in the mid-20th century until grammarians feared over-saturation. Today's rules are more flexible than most grammar rules, allowing the author to determine whether hyphens would aid in clarity or not. Consider the following:

   - *Their company is ready to begin the government-mandated program.*
   - *Are you going to write a getting-ready-for-vacation list?*
     Note: Do not hyphenate compound words that include an –ly adverb.
   - *She has a beautifully decorated library.*
     It's interesting to note, too, that words in the English language often walk a similar trajectory from two words to hyphenated words to a single word. Consider on site → on-site → onsite.

6. The **apostrophe** is used for only two purposes: (1) to show possession and (2) to show something is missing. For possession, the apostrophe goes before the *s* when the subject is singular and after the *s* when the subject is plural. Use only an apostrophe for subjects that are singular but end in *s*.

   - *The dog's bowl is overflowing.* (one dog = 's)
   - *Leia has three cats, and her cats' bowl is often empty.* (multiple cats = s')
   - *Charles' laugh is infectious.*
     Do not use an apostrophe to form a plural noun, such as the *1950's* (correct: *1950s*) or *Saturday's* (correct: *Saturdays*) or *MD's* (correct: *MDs*). An exception is allowed if an

apostrophe is necessary for clarity: *He has trouble pronouncing e's and i's* would be difficult to read without the apostrophes.

- *I don't want to leave the house today.* (don't = do not)
- *She wouldn't like it if she knew.* (wouldn't = would not)
- *The '60s were a tumultuous time in American history.* ('60s = 1960s)

7. **Quotation marks** are used (1) with direct quotes and (2) with the titles of shorter works. Remember that commas and periods always go inside quotation marks, whether the quote is a single word or a longer sentence.

   - *"I thought you were ready to go," he said.*
   - *She has often wondered whether her children understand the meaning of the word "literally."*
   - *Have you read the Robert Frost poem "Stopping by Woods on a Snowy Evening"?*
   - *Her grandmother loves to sing "Amazing Grace" on Sunday mornings.*

     When writing the titles of longer works, such as a novel, newspaper, or magazine, use italics: *The Red Pony, The Oregonian, Better Homes & Gardens.*

8. The **ellipsis** is a set of three periods used (1) to show missing material or (2) to suggest a pause or suspenseful moment. Avoid the second use in professional or academic writing.

   - *In* A Reader's Guide to James Joyce, *William Tindall supports the idea: "Stephen's theory and this manuscript give us a profitable way of approaching Joyce's works, all of which ... may be thought of as epiphanies, Dubliners, especially."*
     When beginning a quote partway into a sentence,

substitute a capital letter with brackets rather than using an ellipsis:

- "[T]his manuscript give[s] us a profitable way of approaching Joyce's works, all of which ... may be thought of as epiphanies, Dubliners, especially."

Most formatting styles do not require an ellipsis if you end a quote before the sentence is completed, but MLA does. Here is what that would look like, including the final period:

- "[T]his manuscript give[s] us a profitable way of approaching Joyce's works, all of which ... may be thought of as epiphanies ... ."

9. The **bracket** is used for one of two purposes: (1) for clarity in a direct quotation or (2) when you have a parenthetical within a parenthetical.

    - "One or more of [Joyce's] books commonly appears in lists of the 'hundred best books,' along with works of Sophocles, Homer, and Dante," Tindall writes.
    - C. S. Lewis is the most widely published Christian apologist of the 20th century (consider Alister McGrath's award-winning biography [2013]).

10. The **slash** is used to show a line break in poetry or, on occasion, to serve as shorthand for *or* or *and*.

    - "April is the cruelest month, breeding / Lilacs out of the dead land, mixing / Memory and desire, stirring / Dull roots with spring rain. / Winter kept us warm, covering / Earth in forgetful snow, feeding / A little life with dried tubers," writes T. S. Eliot in his poem "The Waste Land."
    - The instructions said that it was fine to arrive with a pen and/or pencil for the exam.

COMMON ERRORS:

- **Placing commas according to rhythm or instinct rather than adhering to the simple math.** Each time you consider using a comma, ask yourself which of the six comma rules it adheres to. If you are unable to answer, skip the comma.
- **Assuming that a comma alone is enough to connect two sentences in place of a period.** In order to use a comma, you must follow the equation of *comma + FANBOYS conjunction*.
- **Using a semicolon without a complete sentence on either side.** Remember the simple math of a sentence *(subject + verb)*, and be sure you have the correct math both before and after the semicolon before using it to replace a period.
- **Using a colon without a prior complete sentence**. A colon is not necessary every time you have a list; it is only used with a complete sentence in order to introduce what follows. In the following sentence, a colon not only is not needed but would be incorrect if inserted before the list: *I am headed to the story to pick up bananas, soy milk, and chicken.*
- **Overusing the dash.** Remember to use the dash wisely and sparingly.
- **Typing a single hyphen for a dash.** The hyphen is the shorter line (-) and the dash is the longer line formed by typing two hyphens in a row (–).
- **Using the apostrophe to form plural nouns**: *the Smiths'*, for example. If you are referring to *the Smiths' home*, then use the apostrophe. If you are only referring to the family, the apostrophe is not needed. Avoid using an apostrophe with decades as well: *the 1920's* is incorrect. Consider how lopsided it would look with the apostrophe correctly placed to show am omission at the beginning as well: *the '20's*. Instead use the apostrophe only for the omission: *the '20s*.
- **Placing a comma or period on the outside of the quotation**

marks, which is a rule that still holds in Britain but not in the United States.

- *She ran the race like a "warrior", as her mother used to say.* (British)
- *She ran the race like a "warrior," as her mother used to say.* (American)

EXERCISES:

Exercise 4.1

Insert commas in the following sentences as needed.

1. The first-grade teacher heard the children bickering in the hallway so she hurried to the doorway to see what was the matter.
2. When I go to the mall tomorrow I will be shopping for tennis shoes jeans and T-shirts.
3. Elevators have always frightened her a little but she tries to hide her fear from other people.
4. Those young hairy Hereford cows apparently have not yet shed their winter coats.
5. If we buy lemons and avocadoes will you help me make guacamole?
6. She wants to go to the beach tomorrow too.
7. Mr. Tang will you explain that again please?
8. I would like to buy a large coffee but I might not finish it tonight.
9. "Tell me why" the child begged.
10. Their family has traveled to Oregon Washington and Idaho but they have never been to the East Coast.

Exercise 4.2

Insert punctuation in the following sentences as needed.

1. I wonder whether their new kitten the black one with the white stripe will fully recover from his cold.
2. His grandchildren often leave sticky fingered heart felt gifts for him when they visit.
3. What time will the airplane land Janet asked.
4. I would like to bake a banana bread this afternoon but I am concerned that it is too hot outside to heat the oven.
5. Those examples will work just fine the librarian explained.
6. I hope yesterdays mess an unfortunate pile of melted crayons from an experiment gone awry didn't stain your carpet too badly.
7. She didnt expect to hear from her 15 year old son until the end of the week.
8. Will your father in law want to eat with us?
9. He jogged to the mailbox three days worth of mail made it difficult to jog home.
10. The trees shed their leaves early this year yellows oranges reds and purples that colored the hillsides beautifully before they fell.

Exercise 4.3

Find and correct 10 errors in the following paragraph.

When Eloise joined the womens cross country team she did not expect a complete transformation of how she moved her arms and legs when she ran. As a long-time soccer player Eloise knew she had excellent endurance and she had always been proud of her ability to keep running long after her teammates had tired. But on the first day of practice the cross country coach called her over and asked her to relax her hands drop her shoulders and move her arms to the front rather than across her body. At first the changes felt awkward and Eloise could feel herself wanting to revert back to the way she had always run. But after she had practiced the new form for a week or two, she realized that she was running faster longer and stronger than she ever had before.

ANSWER KEY:

Answer Key Exercise 4.1

1. The first-grade teacher heard the children bickering in the hallway, so she hurried to the doorway to see what was the matter.
2. When I go to the mall tomorrow, I will be shopping for tennis shoes, jeans, and T-shirts.
3. Elevators have always frightened her a little, but she tries to hide her fear from other people.
4. Those young, hairy, Hereford cows apparently have not yet shed their winter coats.
5. If we buy lemons and avocadoes, will you help me make guacamole?
6. She wants to go to the beach tomorrow, too.
7. Mr. Tang, will you explain that again, please?
8. I would like to buy a large coffee, but I might not finish it tonight.
9. "Tell me why," the child begged.
10. Their family has traveled to Oregon, Washington, and Idaho, but they have never been to the East Coast.

Answer Key Exercise 4.2

1. I wonder whether their new kitten (the black one with the white stripe) will fully recover from his cold.
2. His grandchildren often leave sticky-fingered, heart-felt gifts for him when they visit.
3. "What time will the airplane land?" Janet asked.
4. I would like to bake a banana bread this afternoon, but I am concerned that it is too hot outside to heat the oven.
5. "Those examples will work just fine," the librarian explained.
6. I hope yesterday's mess — an unfortunate pile of melted crayons from an experiment gone awry — didn't stain your carpet too badly.
7. She didn't expect to hear from her 15-year-old son until the end of the week.
8. Will your father-in-law want to eat with us?
9. He jogged to the mailbox; three days worth of mail made it difficult to jog home.
10. The trees shed their leaves early this year: yellows, oranges, reds, and purples that colored the hillsides beautifully before they fell.

Answer key Exercise 4.3

Find and correct 10 errors in the following paragraph.

When Eloise joined the women's cross country team, she did not expect a complete transformation of how she moved her arms and legs when she ran. As a long-time soccer player, Eloise knew she had excellent endurance, and she had always been proud of her ability to keep running long after her teammates had tired. But on the first day of practice, the cross country coach called her over and asked her to relax her hands, drop her shoulders, and move her arms to the front rather than across her body. At first the changes felt awkward, and Eloise could feel herself wanting to revert back to the way she had always run. But after she had practiced the new form for a week or two, she realized that she was running faster, longer, and stronger than she ever had before.

CHAPTER 5.

EIGHT PARTS OF SPEECH

The eight parts of speech in the English language determine how a word is functioning in a sentence both in terms of the simple math and in terms of the word's meaning. [Image: JJ Ying | Unsplash]

DEFINITIONS TO REMEMBER:

- **Verb** = action

- **Noun** = a person, place, or thing
- **Pronoun** = takes the place of a noun
- **Adjective** = modifies a noun
- **Adverb** = typically modifies a verb
- **Preposition** = shows relationship between a noun and another word
- **Conjunction** = links different parts of a sentence together
- **Interjection** = an exclamation

RULES TO REMEMBER:

1. The noun that a pronoun replaces is called the **antecedent** of the pronoun. For example, in the sentence *The dog ate his food*, *dog* is the antecedent of the pronoun *his*.

   - *Whenever Jamie arrives in the classroom, she smiles broadly and plops her books in a pile at one of the front-row desks.* (antecedent of *she* = Jamie)

> "More than your background, education, title, or credentials, your ability to communicate clearly, thoughtfully, and without careless errors tells me how much you respect your work, your ideas, and your peers." *Tiffany Butler, Principal, Whole Brain Creative*

2. A **subject pronoun** includes *I, we, you, he, she,* and *they,* and will often be the main subject of the sentence.

   - *We ran as quickly as we could.* (*we* = subject pronoun)

3. An **object pronoun** is the object of the verb, which means

the action happens *to* the pronoun rather than *by* the pronoun.

- *She decided to write it down before she could forget.* (*she* = subject pronoun; *it* = object pronoun)

4. Most **indefinite pronouns** require a singular verb: *anyone, no one, someone, everyone, anybody, nobody, somebody, everybody, anything, nothing, something, everything, either, another, each, one,* and *any*.

    - <u>Everything</u> *is going to be just fine.*
    - <u>Either is</u> *fine with me.*

5. **Reflexive pronouns** include *myself, ourselves, yourself, yourselves, himself, herself, itself,* and *themselves*. Reflexive pronouns can never replace the subject of a sentence.

    - *I decided to sew the button on* <u>myself</u> *rather than ask him to do it for me.*
    - *He drove* <u>himself</u> *to the airport.*

6. **Possessive pronouns** include *my, mine, our, ours, your, yours, his, her, hers, its, their, theirs,* and *whose*. Possessive pronouns replace possessive nouns (*his car* instead of *Luke's car*), and possessive pronouns never take apostrophes.

    - <u>Her</u> *chair has violet flowers stitched across the surface.*
    - *Is this* <u>your</u> *pen?*

7. **Relative pronouns** include *that, which, who, whom, whoever, whomever, whose,* and *what*. *Who* is a subject pronoun, which means it can be the subject of a sentence: *Who is riding the bike this morning? Whom* is an object pronoun, which means it is the direct or indirect object of the verb or a preposition: *For whom did you bring flowers today?* While we

often ignore *whom* in spoken speech, we do not in written English. When in doubt, substitute *he* or *him* for the relative pronoun to see which sounds correct to you:

- *Who/whom did you help move last week?* (1) Change the question to a statement: *You helped who/whom move last week.* (2) Substitute the personal pronouns *he* and *him*: *You helped he move last week* or *You helped him move last week.* (3) If *he* sounds correct, the answer is *who*; if *him* sounds correct, the answer is *whom*: *Whom did you help move last week?*

- *Who* begins a clause that refers to people, *that* begins a clause that refers to a thing, and *which* begins a clause that refers to a thing and that is preceded by a comma:

    - *Margaret is the babysitter who always brings candy when she visits.*
    - *I am going to stand under the tree that has green leaves and wide branches.*
    - *He asked me to meet him near our neighbor's fence, which is listing to one side and badly in need of repair.*

8. **Demonstrative pronouns** include *this, that, these,* and *those.* Be careful of using a demonstrative pronoun without ensuring that your reader clearly understands what antecedent it refers to.

    - Unclear: <u>This</u> *is my favorite.*
      Revised: <u>This</u> *website is my favorite.*
    - Unclear: <u>Those</u> *are the tools that we need.*
      Revised: <u>Those</u> *written exercises are the tools that we need.*

9. **Adjectives** typically answer questions like *which one? what kind?* and *how many?*

- He swallows <u>14</u> <u>blue</u> and <u>purple</u> vitamins every morning.
- Her first horse was <u>a flaxen-maned</u>, <u>chestnut</u> <u>Arabian</u> mare.

10. **Adverbs** can modify a verb, adjective, or additional adverb. The easiest rule to remember is that they typically modify verbs and often end with –ly.

    - She ran <u>quickly</u> across the field.
    - The eagle swooped down <u>suddenly</u> and snatched the field mouse with its talons.

11. **Prepositional phrases** often tell where or when and show relationship. Remember that a main subject will never fall within a prepositional phrase.

    - I hope you will remember to roll the sheets <u>in a neat bundle</u> before you pack them <u>in that box</u>.
    - The sky is blue <u>with purple streaks</u> tonight.

12. **Conjunctions** can be coordinating, correlating, and subordinating.

    - **Coordinating conjunctions** include the seven conjunctions often remembered by the acronym FANBOYS: *for, and, nor, but, or, yet, so*. These conjunctions link equal elements in a sentence.

        - The bird flew into my yard, <u>and</u> it landed on my birdbath.

    - **Correlative conjunctions** are used in pairs to connect words or phrases of equal grammatical value: *as...as, either...or, neither...nor, both...and*. Be sure the two parts of the pair are grammatically parallel.

        - She plans to spend her Saturday <u>either</u> working in the yard <u>or</u> cleaning the kitchen cabinets.

- **Subordinating conjunctions** are used to demonstrate that the meaning of one phrase in a sentence is subordinate to another. Subordinating conjunctions include *after, although, because, before, since, where, while,* and many more.

  - *<u>Because</u> his stomach is still hurting, he will be an hour or two late to the meeting this morning.*
  - *We will plan to have dinner at 8 p.m. tonight <u>since</u> everyone will be home from meetings by then.*

13. **Interjections** are single words that express a sudden burst of emotion, such as *oh, yeah, shhh, yes, ha,* or *oops*. Interjections are frequent in colloquial speech but should be avoided in professional or academic writing.

COMMON ERRORS:

- **Relying on instinct rather than identifying the part of speech.** Once you learn to identify the eight parts of speech, use that knowledge to determine whether a sentence you have written is achieving the depth of meaning that you intend.

- **Assuming that the rules of the English language are subjective and ever-changing.** English teachers can be subjective, but the rules are not. And while the rules may change over time, that change is typically painstakingly slow. The rules are finite and objective, and the internet allows you immediate access to them. When in doubt, look it up.

- **Trusting your ear to know best.** If you grew up in a home where everyone spoke proper English and you surround yourself now with people who speak proper English, your innate sense of the mathematics of language may be excellent. But must of us have not been so fortunate. Colloquial or spoken English typically breaks rules where written English cannot. Learn the simple math so your written English always achieves the effect you intend.

EXERCISES:

Exercise 5.1

Identify and correct the errors in the following sentences.

1. Her and my uncle have been married for 10 years now.
2. My children and me are ready for an adventure this summer.
3. Will you please send the email to Clarence or I as soon as you're able?
4. She has never been one of those people that slinks into the room.
5. I asked him to sit in the chair which is closest to the stage.
6. This past year has been financially difficult for my husband and I.
7. Every time I contact that company, they give me the run-around.
8. Their family plans to meet at the campsite which is surrounded by Douglas firs.
9. Arnold gave his snack to the kid that is on his right.
10. Have you decided who you will choose for the A team?

Exercise 5.2

Identify and correct the errors in the following sentences.

1. I have never understood why my girlfriend and me were not invited to his wedding.
2. Do you know whom wrote that beautiful love poem?
3. She is the kind of person for who family will always come first.
4. You have to believe in you if you hope to do well.

5. Maria sat with her legs neatly crossed as she waited for her brother and I.
6. The bushes which are browning on the edges are the ones we will need to replace next.
7. If we finish our work quick, we can go to the mall.
8. He always plays good in the second half of the competition.
9. Who are you waiting for?
10. Boaz will either run into the bushes or jumping into my arms.

Exercise 5.3

Identify and correct the errors in the following paragraph.

When Alicia visited the Chicago Art Institute, she was surprised to see so many themed exhibits which were available for viewing only during the summer months. She wanted to get the most for her money, so she looked for a museum aide that would be able to answer her questions. Once she found a young woman willing to help, she asked whether she should take the stairs or ride the escalator. The young woman, which wore a bright blue museum jacket and nametag, suggested that Alicia join her in a private elevator. Together they rode to the contemporary exhibit on the third floor, and Alicia and her strolled through the artwork together. Alicia was surprised to learn about the donors who the woman described, and she wondered what kind of people had that kind of money to spare. Her and the aide stopped in front of a Picasso display. Alicia wanted to move slow through the exhibit, but the woman encouraged her to walk more quickly because there was still so much more to see. As she turned a corner, Alicia paused to admire a sculpture which was perched on the edge of a stairwell. When the aide and her parted ways just before lunch, Alicia thanked her new friend for a morning well spent.

ANSWER KEY:

Answer Key Exercise 5.1

1. <u>She</u> and my uncle have been married for 10 years now.
2. My children and <u>I</u> are ready for an adventure this summer.
3. Will you please send the email to Clarence or <u>me</u> as soon as you're able?
4. She has never been one of those people <u>who</u> slinks into the room.
5. I asked him to sit in the chair <u>that</u> is closest to the stage.
6. This past year has been financially difficult for my husband and <u>me</u>.
7. Every time I contact that company, <u>the operator gives</u> me the runaround.
8. Their family plans to meet at the campsite <u>that</u> is surrounded by Douglas firs.
9. Arnold gave his snack to the kid <u>who</u> is on his right.
10. Have you decided <u>whom</u> you will choose for the A team?

Answer Key Exercise 5.2

1. I have never understood why my girlfriend and <u>I</u> were not invited to his wedding.
2. Do you know <u>who</u> wrote that beautiful love poem?
3. She is the kind of person for <u>whom</u> family will always come first.
4. You have to believe in <u>yourself</u> if you hope to do well.
5. Maria sat with her legs neatly crossed as she waited for her brother and <u>me</u>.
6. The bushes <u>that</u> are browning on the edges are the ones we will need to replace next.
7. If we finish our work <u>quickly</u>, we can go to the mall.

8. He always plays *well* in the second half of the competition.
9. *Whom* are you waiting for?
10. Boaz will either run into the bushes or <u>jump</u> into my arms.

Answer Key Exercise 5.3

When Alicia visited the Chicago Art Institute, she was surprised to see so many themed exhibits <u>that</u> were available for viewing only during the summer months. She wanted to get the most for her money, so she looked for a museum aide <u>who</u> would be able to answer her questions. Once she found a young woman willing to help, <u>Alicia</u> asked whether she should take the stairs or ride the escalator. The young woman, <u>who</u> wore a bright blue museum jacket and nametag, suggested that Alicia join her in a private elevator. Together they rode to the contemporary exhibit on the third floor, and Alicia and <u>she</u> strolled through the artwork together. Alicia was surprised to learn about the donors <u>whom</u> the woman described, and she wondered what kind of people had that kind of money to spare. <u>She</u> and the aide stopped in front of a Picasso display. Alicia wanted to move <u>slowly</u> through the exhibit, but the woman encouraged her to walk more quickly because there was still so much more to see. As she turned a corner, Alicia paused to admire a sculpture <u>that</u> was perched on the edge of a stairwell. When the aide and <u>she</u> parted ways just before lunch, Alicia thanked her new friend for a morning well spent.

CHAPTER 6.

CONSISTENCY

The key to clarity at the sentence level is to choose with intention, and then be consistent with the choices you make. [Image: Mike Tinnion | Unsplash]

DEFINITIONS TO REMEMBER:

- **Verb Tense:** choose with intention, and then be consistent.
- **Pronoun Reference:** be sure the pronoun and its antecedent always match.

- **Collective Nouns:** choose with intention, and then be consistent.
- **Modifiers:** be sure the modifier and its antecedent are as close together as possible.

RULES TO REMEMBER:

1. If you choose to use past **tense**, stay consistently in past tense. If you choose to use present tense, stay consistently in present tense. When you alternate between the two, your readers will be confused and unsure of your meaning. Consider the following:

    - *The author <u>argues</u> a strong cause, <u>listed</u> several notable contemporaries, and <u>promises</u> to be remembered for her work.*
    Argues and *promises* are present tense verbs, but *listed* is in the past tense. To ensure consistency, change *listed* to *lists*.

    - *Timothy <u>marched</u> past the line of waiting customers, straight to the counter. He <u>shouts</u> at the woman that he wants a refund. Then he <u>emptied</u> his bag onto the counter to show her the broken device.*
    Here, again, the verbs alternate between past and present tense. *Marched* and *emptied* are in past tense, while *shouts* is in present tense. To ensure consistency, change *shouts* to *shouted*.

2. Any time you use a **pronoun**, make sure you can draw a straight and clear line to its antecedent so your readers are never left wondering. Be sure, too, that the pronoun and antecedent are either both plural or both singular.

    - *When <u>a club member</u> does not want to pay <u>their</u> dues, we will need to impose a penalty.*
    A club member is singular, which means the pronoun *their* must be singular as well. Revised: *When <u>a club member</u> does*

not want to pay <u>his or her</u> dues, we will need to impose a penalty.

- *<u>Everyone</u> should cast <u>their</u> own vote.*
  Everyone is a singular collective noun, which means *their* must be singular as well. Revised: *<u>Everyone</u> should cast <u>his or her</u> own vote.* If *his or her* sounds cumbersome, another fix is to make the antecedent plural so *their* works as a plural pronoun: *<u>All members</u> should cast <u>their</u> own votes.*

3. Many **collective nouns** can be either singular or plural depending on the context. Choose intentionally, and be consistent once you choose. When in doubt, keep collective nouns singular.

   - *The faculty is divided into six colleges within the larger university.*
     In this example, *faculty* functions as a singular collective noun. But consider this example: *The faculty are each expected to complete the survey by Friday.* Here *faculty* functions as a plural collective noun. Either is fine, but be sure to be consistent throughout a single work so your readers are not confused. Other examples of collective nouns include *jury, media collective, department, flock, herd, hive, army,* and *catch.*

4. A **misplaced modifier** is a modifier that is so far from the noun it modifies that your readers could mistakenly assume that it is modifying another part of the sentence. To avoid confusion, always ensure that the modifier is placed as close to its antecedent as possible.

   - *Bathed in brandy, the church ladies enjoyed the baked pears.* Revised: *The church ladies enjoyed the baked pears that were bathed in brandy.*
   - *Eagerly awaiting her trip, Bertha's suitcase was placed by*

Bertha on the top of the stairs.
Revised: *Eagerly awaiting her trip, Bertha placed her suitcase on the top of the stairs.*

○ *The couple bought a pony for their daughter named Oreo.*
Revised: *The couple bought a pony named Oreo for their daughter.*

COMMON ERRORS:

- **Assuming that writing is a one-step process, rather than recognizing the importance of revision.** Most of the sentence equation errors discussed in Part 1 are difficult to catch without a careful second or third reading. Always save time to reread your work, whether you have written a text, an email, a letter to a client, or a final paper for a course.

- **Allowing yourself to be distracted by sentence-level math when you are writing a first draft.** When you sit down to draft, imagine the person or people you are writing to and simply talk to them without worrying about grammatical errors. Allow the revision process to catch those errors rather than risking writer's block by second-guessing yourself.

- **Assuming that your readers will understand what you mean.** Never assume. Chances are they will assume something you never imagined, and your chance at effective communication will be lost.

> "Using clear and concise writing ensures that the customers we serve understand what we expect of them and what they can expect of us. Avoiding confusion saves time and has the added benefit of helping employers avoid litigation." *Joel D. Moore, Graduate Admissions Counselor*

EXERCISES:

Exercise 6.1

Find and correct the errors in the following sentences.

1. Anyone who wants to go to college can put together a plan that they will hold to until their goal is accomplished.
2. Raul reclined in the lawn chair, opened his magazine wide, and promptly falls sound asleep in the sun.
3. The team played their best players in the first three innings.
4. Why won't the restaurant advertise what time they open?
5. Each one of the kids has their own unique personality.
6. The book reads like a fast-paced novel. The author closed each chapter with a cliff-hanger that compels readers to keep reading.
7. The neighborhood church serves their community with joy and enthusiasm.
8. I drank my coffee slowly. It burns my mouth if I drink too quickly.
9. When you answer the question, be sure to select the person who had the greatest impact with their intellectual contributions.
10. This kind of heat can impact a person's ability to think as you try to do homework.

Exercise 6.2

Find and correct the errors in the following sentences.

1. At the circus, we bought hot dogs for the children covered in ketchup.
2. Reading the restrictions sign, the baby was not permitted to join her mother in the hotel hot tub.

3. With carefully gelled hair, the Ford F150 had its tires changed by the auto mechanic.
4. While eating chicken soup, the parakeet swooped over Josephine's head.
5. Waving in the wind, the old woman watched the beautiful willow tree.
6. Driving along the one-lane highway, the Dalmatian leaned his head out of Mark's passenger window.
7. With deep wrinkles etched in her cheeks, the magazine editor proudly ran a story about Eva, a 104-year-old woman who had helped to start the publication many years before.
8. Sun danced across the top of the water as the boy rode his surfboard with red swim trunks.
9. The textbook belonged to Eric with the scientist in a lab coat on the cover.
10. Reaching down, the baby was lifted into the stroller by her nanny.

Exercise 6.3

Find and correct the errors in the following paragraph.

When Zane brought his two year old to the swimming pool for a first lesson last week, he is surprised by the chaos of pre-lesson preparations. With goggles gripped tightly in her fist, another parent's friendly Labrador retriever distracted Emily with her wet kisses. Sprawled across the wet cement floor with her arms wide open to the friendly dog, Zane tried to redirect Emily toward the swimming pool. At the athletic club, they always did a nice job of hiring welcoming, knowledgeable swimming instructors. Once Zane introduced Emily to her teacher, he tries to retreat back to the parents' seating area. A small crowd were gathered, and Zane found a seat among them. Once seated, Emily realized that he had left her and began to cry. Waving with a wide smile on her face, Zane saw that the teacher was looking directly at him and beckoning him to come back. Rising to his feet, Emily reached for her dad as he made his way back to the poolside. For the remainder of the lesson, Zane crouches near the water's edge, encouraging Emily as she laughs and splashes in the water.

ANSWER KEY:

Answer Key Exercise 6.1

1. Anyone who wants to go to college can put together a plan that <u>he or she</u> will hold to until <u>the</u> goal is accomplished.
2. Raul reclined in the lawn chair, opened his magazine wide, and promptly <u>fell</u> sound asleep in the sun.
3. The team played <u>its</u> best players in the first three innings.
4. Why won't the restaurant advertise what time <u>it opens</u>?
5. Each one of the kids has <u>his or her</u> own unique personality.
6. The book reads like a fast-paced novel. The author <u>closes</u> each chapter with a cliff-hanger that compels readers to keep reading.
7. The neighborhood church serves <u>its</u> community with joy and enthusiasm.
8. I <u>drink</u> my coffee slowly. It burns my mouth if I drink too quickly.
9. When you answer the question, be sure to select the person who had the greatest impact with <u>his or her</u> intellectual contributions.
10. This kind of heat can impact <u>your</u> ability to think as you try to do homework.

Answer Key Exercise 6.2

1. At the circus, we bought hot dogs <u>covered in ketchup</u> for the children.

2. Reading the restrictions sign, <u>the mother realized that</u> the baby was not permitted to join her in the hotel hot tub.
3. With carefully gelled hair, <u>the auto mechanic changed the tires of</u> the Ford F150.
4. While <u>Josephine was</u> eating chicken soup, the parakeet swooped over <u>her</u> head.
5. <u>T</u>he old woman watched the beautiful willow tree <u>waving in the wind</u>.
6. Driving along the one-lane highway, <u>Mark drove as</u> the Dalmatian leaned his head out of <u>the</u> passenger window.
7. <u>T</u>he magazine editor proudly ran a story about Eva, a 104-year-old woman <u>with deep wrinkles etched in her cheeks</u> who had helped to start the publication many years before.
8. Sun danced across the top of the water as the boy <u>with red swim trunks</u> rode his surfboard.
9. The textbook <u>with the scientist in a lab coat on the cover</u> belonged to Eric.
10. Reaching down, <u>the nanny lifted</u> the baby into the stroller.

Answer Key Exercise 6.3

When Zane brought his two year old to the swimming pool for a first lesson last week, he <u>was</u> surprised by the chaos of pre-lesson preparations. With goggles gripped tightly in her fist, <u>Emily was distracted by the wet kisses of</u> another parent's friendly Labrador retriever. Zane tried to redirect Emily toward the swimming pool <u>even though she was sprawled across the wet cement floor with her arms wide open to the friendly dog</u>. At the athletic club, <u>the management</u> always did a nice job of hiring welcoming, knowledgeable swimming instructors. Once Zane introduced Emily to her teacher, he <u>tried</u> to retreat back to the parents' seating area. A small crowd <u>was</u> gathered, and Zane found a seat among them. Once <u>Zane was</u> seated, Emily realized that he had left her and began to cry. Waving with a wide smile on her face, the teacher was looking directly at Zane and beckoning him to come back. Rising to his feet, Zane made his way back to the poolside as Emily reached for him. For the remainder of the lesson, Zane crouched near the water's edge, encouraging Emily as she laughed and splashed in the water.

PART II.

THE PARAGRAPH EQUATION

Once you are able to recognize the mathematical pattern of the basic sentence, it is time to move up to the next linguistic equation: the paragraph. I recently opened a new writing class by asking students how many sentences comprise a paragraph. The answers came with as much confidence as they were varied: 3 to 5, 4 to 6, 6 to 8. Students looked at one another with surprise as they waited for me to validate the answer they were taught, but the truth is simple. An effective paragraph must have at least 2 sentences: (1) an effective topic sentence that states the purpose of the paragraph, and (2) clear and specific evidence to support that purpose. The choice between a single sentence providing evidence or multiple sentences providing evidence depends entirely on the writer's purpose and audience. When we complicate the simple math with preferences like 4, 6, or 8, we muddle the simplicity of basic linguistic structure. Equation #2: a topic sentence + evidence = a paragraph.

CHAPTER 7.

TOPIC SENTENCES

Every paragraph must have a topic sentence that clearly states your purpose for that paragraph. [Image: Diego PH | Unsplash]

DEFINITION TO REMEMBER:

- **Topic Sentence = the purpose of your paragraph**

Every paragraph must have a topic sentence that states clearly for your readers the purpose of that specific paragraph. If you do not have a topic sentence, how will your readers understand your intent? If you are unsure what your topic sentence should be, how can you expect your readers to dig through to locate your meaning? If you aren't clear on the purpose of a single paragraph, why have you bothered to include it?

As we move from the sentence equation to the paragraph equation, it is important to recognize that the simple math is equally important at the paragraph level. Just as *subject + verb = sentence*, your readers will expect this equation of each paragraph you write: *topic sentence + evidence = paragraph.*

The easiest place to situate the topic sentence is as the first line of each new paragraph, followed by direct evidence. But you are free to place the topic sentence anywhere that is most effective for your meaning, as long as you have one.

> **"Keep the main thing, the main thing. Use the best words to make your point, rather than the most words. Clear, concise writing is a gift for the reader."** *Heather Rainey, Administrative Assistant, Doctor of Ministry Program*

To write an effective topic sentence, picture your audience sitting beside your desk. If you had to state the purpose of your paragraph in a single sentence to your audience, whether it is a single person or a convention center full of thousands, what would you say? If you are not used to including a topic sentence with each new paragraph you write, save this step for your revision work. Often the topic sentence can be fine-tuned or even added after you have finished writing the draft.

RULES TO REMEMBER:

1. Every paragraph must have a clear topic sentence.
2. The topic sentence must clearly state your purpose for that paragraph.
3. If you have more than one paragraph, the topic sentence must be a single sentence (*subject + verb = sentence*) that both presents your topic for the paragraph and builds on the ideas you have presented already. If you line up your topic sentences, one after the other, are they repetitive of one another? Do the ideas drift forward and back, or does your line of thinking move clear forward to a single main point? Remember, too, that each new topic sentence should relate directly to your overall thesis statement if you are writing an essay.

COMMON ERRORS:

- **Skipping the topic sentence because the meaning is self-evident or implied.** Never assume that your readers are heading in the same direction you are. Instead offer them the simple math necessary to keep your communication clear, concise, and meaningful.
- **Combining the topic sentence with other information**, with an assumption that the readers will understand which is which. Instead include a single clear topic sentence in each new paragraph you write.

EXERCISES:

Exercise 7.1

If you were to write a paragraph about each of the following topics, what would your topic sentence be? How can you ensure that you topic sentence is a clear statement that presents both your topic and your claim about your topic? How can you learn to write topic sentences quickly and efficiently, so it becomes second nature for you?

> Example Topic: *Books*
> Example Topic Sentence: *Because of cost and convenience, online open textbooks will one day replace standard print textbooks.*

1. Cooking
2. Sports
3. My family
4. Medical care
5. Government
6. Computers
7. Children
8. Pets
9. Travel
10. Technology

Exercise 7.2

Find a paragraph you have written in the past week, whether for work, school, or personal use. Was there a topic sentence? If so, what was the topic sentence? Are you confident that your topic sentence clearly presents your purpose for the paragraph? If not, what should your topic sentence be? How will the addition of a clear topic sentence aid your readers?

Exercise 7.3

Consider at least five potential paragraphs that you will need to write in the next week, whether for work, school, or personal use. As in Exercise 7.1, name the topic, and then write a topic sentence that could serve well once you are ready to write your full paragraph.

1.

2.

3.

4.

5.

CHAPTER 8.

EVIDENCE

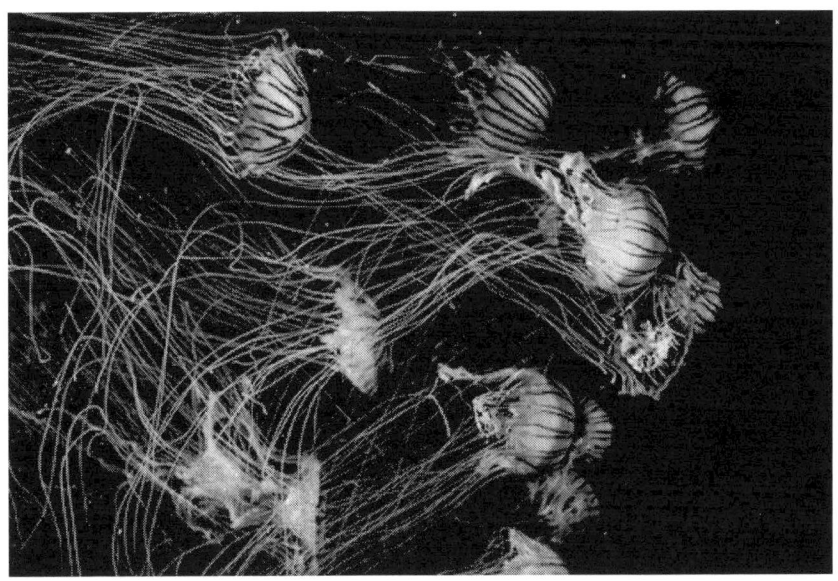

The more specific your evidence is, the more persuasive and memorable your claim will be.
[Image: StockSnap | Pixabay]

DEFINITION TO REMEMBER:

- **Topic Sentence + Evidence = Paragraph**

RULES TO REMEMBER:

1. Once you have decided what *claim* you will make about your *topic*, you must decide what supporting material will best demonstrate to your readers that you have good reason to believe what you do about your subject. Without evidence, you will find yourself merely repeating your ideas.
2. The more specific your *evidence* is, the more persuasive and memorable your claim will be. The key here – regardless of the kind of writing you are doing, whether an anthropology term paper or an email to your boss – is to *show* your readers, rather than merely *tell* them.

"As a social change-agent, I ended up writing and editing policies for a startup charter school. These policies codified our commitment to being a healthy civic partner, protected public assets, and helped clarify – in a time of rapid change and growth – our community expectations." *Kirsten Rayhawk, Board Member, Portland Village School*

Consider, for example, the following paragraph. It begins with a clear *topic sentence*, followed by very specific *evidence*. Take note that the author does not bother to explain and re-explain the ideas (telling), but instead offers specific, visual details (showing) so we readers can better identify with the claims at hand:

- *My oldest son was a daredevil as a child. When he was in second-grade, he was called to the principal's office for encouraging a crowd of boys to toss rocks over the school yard fence at passing cars. When he was in fourth grade, he built a jump for his bike at the neighborhood park and gained so much air that he nearly fractured his spine when he landed. When he as a sophomore in high school, I grounded him for an entire summer after he organized a drag race at the beach and ran our family Jeep directly into oncoming waves. Indeed, life with my spirited oldest son has never been dull.*

3. *Evidence* can mean a number of different kinds of support. *Examples* are just one option. To develop a topic sentence into a full paragraph, you might also include any of the following: *examples, reasons, facts, details, statistics, anecdotes,* or *quotations from experts.*
4. Your *evidence* should always be (1) relevant and unified, (2) specific, (3) adequate, (4) accurate, (5) representative, and (6) if borrowed, properly documented.

COMMON ERRORS:

- **Repeating the topic sentence rather than moving directly into evidence.** If you need to repeat or clarify your topic sentence in order to ensure that your readers understand, rewrite your topic sentence until it is sufficient on its own and you are able to move on to your specific evidence. Consider the person you know who repeats a certain conviction over and over but never offers any evidence. Most of us eventually stop listening, right? Instead offer your readers solid evidence to support your assertions and see what changes you are able to bring about.
- **Including general *always evidence* rather than specific *single-moment evidence*.** If your topic sentence states that a particular author offers an effective new approach to global warming, would it be more effective to wax on about how he *always* writes the most interesting arguments, or would it make more sense to reference specific sources, showing your

readers what you have witnessed rather than merely telling them?

- **Saving evidence for a later paragraph without remembering that every paragraph must adhere to the simple math of** *topic sentence + evidence = paragraph.* If you are writing an academic essay, an email to your boss at work, or a letter to a client, this equation applies to every new paragraph you write.

EXERCISES:

Exercise 8.1

If you were to write a paragraph about each of the following topics from Exercise 7.1, what would your evidence be? How can you ensure that you evidence is clear and specific? How can you learn to think of potential evidence quickly and efficiently, so it becomes second nature for you?

> Example Topic: *Books*
>
> Example Topic Sentence: *Because of cost and convenience, online open textbooks will one day replace standard print textbooks.*
>
> Example Evidence: (1) a free Math 150 textbook versus $140 for a paper copy, (2) the ease of accessing the Math 150 textbook online rather than carrying a heavy paper copy, (3) the cost savings of 30 students x $140 in a single fall course listing.

1. Cooking
2. Sports
3. My family
4. Medical care
5. Government
6. Computers
7. Children
8. Pets

9. Travel
10. Technology

Exercise 8.2

Find a paragraph you have written in the past week, whether for work, school, or personal use. Was there clear evidence to support your topic sentence? If so, what was the evidence? Are you confident that your evidence clearly supported your purpose for the paragraph? Was the evidence as single-moment specific as possible? If not, what changes would you make? How will the addition of clear, specific evidence aid your readers?

Exercise 8.3

Consider at least five potential paragraphs that you will need to write in the next week, whether for work, school, or personal use. As in Exercise 8.1, name the topic, and then list one to three elements of specific evidence for each topic that could serve well once you are ready to write your full paragraph.

1.
2.
3.
4.
5.

CHAPTER 9.

SUMMARY SENTENCES

Rather than serve as a repetition of your topic sentence, a closing summary sentence should summarize your ideas in a way that is unique and meaningful for your readers. [Image: Jakob Owens | Unsplash]

DEFINITION TO REMEMBER:

- **Topic Sentence + Evidence (+ Summary Sentence) = Paragraph**

RULES TO REMEMBER:

1. While a topic sentence and solid evidence are essential parts of any new paragraph, a summary sentence is an optional component worth acknowledging. If the information you are presenting is complex or your paragraph is longer than usual, a summary sentence at the end of the paragraph can be an excellent way to remind your readers of your overall purpose for the paragraph as you prepare to move on to a new point.
2. Rather than serve as a repetition of your topic sentence, a closing summary sentence should summarize your ideas in a way that is unique and meaningful for your readers. Consider the following example:

   - *My doctoral adviser was a difficult woman. When I took a literary criticism course from her, she spent at least a portion of the time grilling me on the merits of my master's degree and whether I should really be sitting in her course. When I walked by her in the hallway on my way to teach, she made a point of looking the other way so she didn't have to engage with me. And when she arrived late and unprepared for my oral exams in April, I knew I was in for a difficult session. It was little consolation to learn years later that she had struggled with an addiction problem during those years; mostly I wondered how such a difficult woman could possibly find joy in the depth and nuance of canonized literature.*

   While the closing summary sentence here echoes some of the language of the topic sentence, it does more than merely repeat.

3. A summary sentence is also an effective way to consistently remind your readers of your paper's overall thesis statement. If you include summary sentences consistently at the close of each paragraph, use that final sentence to clearly connect the evidence of that specific paragraph to the thesis of your paper.
4. If you are writing a paragraph to a boss or client, a summary sentence is an effective way to remind your readers of how your ideas relate specifically to their needs or concerns.

COMMON ERRORS:

- **Including a summary sentence that is repetitive of information already offered** and adds nothing to further the discussion. Remember that the summary sentence is optional; use it only when it strengthens your argument rather than waters it down.

> *"In my cross-cultural context, my writing must be clear and concise. I focus on 'write-bites' that are easily translated and transferable." Dr. David Toth, Missionary*

- **Neglecting to remind readers of the larger purpose of the overall paper.** If you are going to include a summary sentence at the end of each paragraph, let it serve a robust purpose for you.

- **Using the summary sentence to introduce the next paragraph.** While some English teachers teach this method as a means of transitioning from one idea to the next, it rarely works. The formula your readers will expect to see in each paragraph you write is this: *topic sentence + evidence (+ optional summary sentence) = paragraph.* When you introduce new information without addressing it fully, your ideas will begin to sound scattered and diluted. Hold to the simple math instead.

EXERCISES:

Exercise 9.1

Choose 5 of the 10 topics in Exercise 7.1 and Exercise 8.1. Record the topic of each paragraph, and write a summary sentence on the lines below. Does the additional summary strengthen or weaken your overall paragraph? Why?

1.
2.
3.
4.
5.

Exercise 9.2

Consider at least five paragraphs you have written in the past week, whether for work, school, or personal use. Did you include a summary sentence? Why or why not? Write a summary sentence for those you did not choose to write initially and decide whether the additional summary strengthens or weakens your argument. Record the topic of each paragraph and the summary sentence on the lines below.

1.
2.
3.
4.
5.

Exercise 9.3

Choose one of the topics you used for Exercise 8.3 and write a summary sentence to conclude the paragraph. Do you anticipate a stronger paragraph with or without the summary sentence? Why?

PART III.

THE ESSAY EQUATION

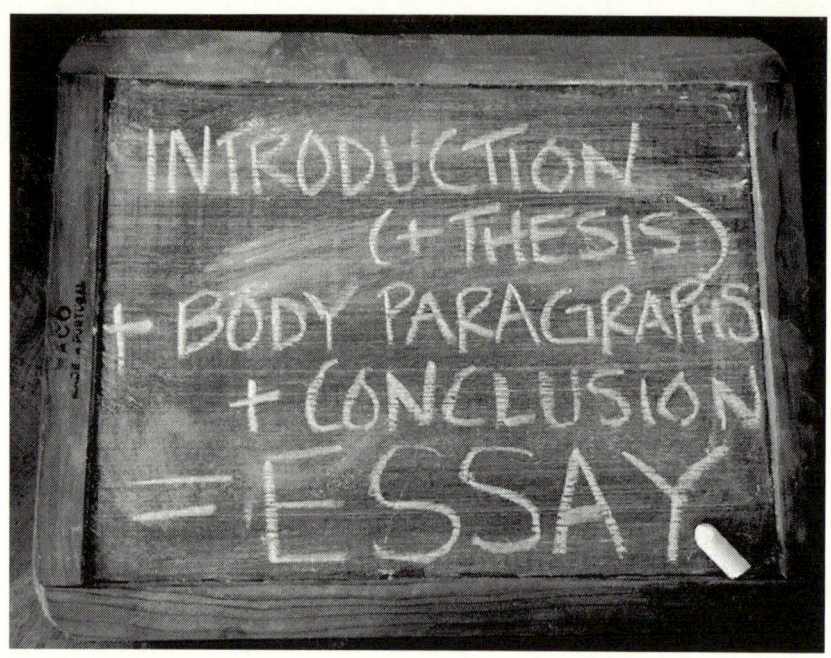

Much as an understanding of addition and subtraction is essential if we hope to multiply and divide numbers successfully, we must have a solid understanding of (1) the sentence equation and (2) the paragraph equation before we can write an effective and meaningful essay. Writers who sit frozen before a blinking cursor, who struggle to keep their ideas from meandering in circles, and who wonder with frustration why their readers can't pinpoint their purpose have forgotten the simple linguistic equation for an effective essay. Once you understand the math, there is no reason for writer's block or misunderstood intentions: Simply apply the math. For those of you who balk at the restrictiveness of a mathematical essay structure, consider it this way: The essay equation provides the backbone that your readers will naturally seek. Once you have the backbone in place, be as creative as your purpose and audience will allow. Equation #3: an introduction + body paragraphs + a conclusion = an essay.

CHAPTER 10.

THESIS STATEMENTS

The thesis statement should be a single, concise sentence. An effective thesis statement has two parts: (1) the topic and (2) your claim about the topic. [Image: Edu Lauton | Unsplash]

DEFINITION TO REMEMBER:

- **Thesis = Topic + Claim**

RULES TO REMEMBER:

1. A *thesis statement* is the main idea or subject of your paper, while a topic sentence is the main idea of a single paragraph. Sometimes the thesis may develop in your mind early in the writing process, and sometimes it will become more clear or shift as you work through the writing process.
2. The thesis statement should be a single, concise sentence. An effective thesis statement has two parts: (1) the topic and (2) your claim about the topic.
3. Your thesis is a contract that you establish with your readers. The voice, tone, assurances, and promises of your thesis must continue throughout the essay.
4. An effective thesis statement should be as specific as possible and be limited enough to make it manageable. Keep your thesis statement specific enough to be adequately discussed within the length of your paper. If a thesis statement is too general or vague, it can be difficult to decide what to write about.
5. Be wary of absolute words like *all, none, everyone, no one, always, never* in your thesis statement. If a reader can think of an exception to your absolute statement, he or she may set your entire argument aside. Be careful, too, to avoid claims that are too over-arching and, therefore, suspect.
6. Your thesis should serve as an umbrella for the essay that follows. Every topic sentence for each of the body paragraphs must fit neatly beneath the umbrella, just as every item of evidence also must fit. If anything does not fit under the umbrella of your thesis, revise accordingly to either broaden or narrow your umbrella until the simple math works.
7. To compose an effective thesis statement, follow these three steps:

    - **Restate your topic as a question.** If, for example, your topic is about the health and care of domestic cats, you might restate your topic as follows: *Should domestic cats be permitted to roam freely in residential neighborhoods?* Do you see how this restatement begins to give both your research and your writing better purpose?

- **Answer your question with a single-sentence claim.** An effective thesis statement (1) announces a topic and (2) states a claim. What assertion will you make about your topic and why? To answer our domestic cat question, we might assert the following: *Domestic cats should only be permitted to roam freely in residential neighborhoods if they meet specific county-designated standards.*

- **Focus your thesis.** Remember that the more specific you are, the easier it will be to effectively discuss and prove your thesis: *Domestic cats should only be permitted to roam freely in residential neighborhoods if they have a chip inserted that identifies their home, homeowner, and vaccination record.*

COMMON ERRORS:

- **Assuming that the implied focus of an introduction is enough.** Every essay must have a clear, concise thesis statement; never assume that your readers understand your intentions.

> **"Write succinctly. There is a better chance people will read and appreciate your thoughts."** *Dr. Aimee Stone Cooper, Pastor*

- **Including a thesis that does not make a claim.** With the advent of the internet, gone are the days when informational papers were a necessary exercise. Because most information is available at the touch of an app, your focus must be on the claim you intend to make about the topic you have chosen.

- **Presenting a thesis that is too broad or too narrow.** While the line between the two can be tenuous and difficult to locate, it is worth the effort. When a thesis is too broad, it is difficult to argue adequately without leaving notable holes in your rationale; when a thesis is too narrow, it can be challenging to find much at all to say to one another.

- **Neglecting to revise the thesis umbrella as the project unfolds.** The more flexible you are, the more successful your end result will be.

EXERCISES:

Exercise 10.1

Find three thesis statements from papers you have written in the past and list them here. If you walk each through the three-step process on item 6 above, how would each one fare? What changes would you make, and why?

1.

2.

3.

Exercise 10.2

Select one thesis from 10.1. Draw or download an umbrella image, and write your thesis on or above the umbrella. Next, write one topic sentence from each paragraph of your essay vertically beneath the umbrella. Keep all information beneath the shape of the umbrella. As you consider your ideas, what revisions do you need to make? Do you need to broaden your thesis in order to encompass all that falls beneath? Or do you need to focus your thesis better, so your readers are able to immediately see the logic of the ideas that come under the umbrella? Are there topics under the umbrella that could be saved for another essay? Do you need additional evidence under the umbrella to strengthen your overall claim?

Exercise 10.3

Consider an essay or writing assignment you will need to complete in the next week, whether for school, work, or home. What is the topic? What is your claim about the topic? What specific evidence will you include? What will your thesis statement be? Use the progression below to aid your thinking:

Topic → Claim → Evidence → Thesis

CHAPTER 11.

INTRODUCTIONS

First impressions are critical. If you want your readers to continue reading, you must capture their attention, present yourself as reasonably authoritative, and offer a clear sense of purpose – all in your introductory paragraph. [Image: Ashim D'Silva | Unsplash]

DEFINITION TO REMEMBER:

- **Catchy First Line + Inspiration + Thesis = Introduction**

RULES TO REMEMBER:

1. First impressions are critical. If you want your readers to continue reading, you must capture their attention, present yourself as reasonably authoritative, and offer a clear sense of purpose – all in your introductory paragraph.
2. A **catchy first line** is essential. If humor is appropriate to your purpose and audience, use it. If a question might help draw your readers in, open with one. Remember that your first line and your thesis statement are typically not the same; most essays open with a catchy first line, with the thesis statement falling somewhere near the end of the first paragraph. Your first line does not need to carry the weight of a thesis statement, so have fun with it. Keep it short, and keep your readers wondering so they will choose to read on.

Consider the following first lines. Would you keep reading? Why or why not?

- It was a morning that would never end.
- Ralph fell sideways.
- When the sun set over the national forest on May 17, 1980, no one realized the enormity of what the next day would bring.
- Saturdays were chicken-soup-making days, which meant Beulah was required to select the best chicken from the coop, snap its neck with a firm twist, and pluck feather after feather from the warm skin.
- Politicians rarely listen well.
- I was done.
- Thirty-two emails later, the deal was signed.
- When Steve Jobs introduced the iPhone to the world in June 2007, everything changed.

- They spent the first two years of their marriage in a Japanese internment camp in northern Washington state.
- The root system of the Douglas fir is surprisingly shallow for a tree that often grows to more than 70 feet tall.

3. Without **inspiration**, you will have a difficult time convincing your readers that they should be inspired to read further. If you want your readers to be engaged, you must be energetic about the ideas you want to communicate, and that energy should show through in your very first opening lines. What excites or interests you about this topic? Should you open with a particularly inviting story, or a surprising fact, or a compelling question? How will you inspire your readers to join you for this journey? Consider the following options to bring life and energy to your introduction:

    - a related story
    - a provocative question or series of questions
    - a hypothetical scenario
    - a surprising fact or series of facts
    - an engaging direct quotation
    - a striking statement
    - background information or context
    - an opposing argument
    - the who, what, where, when, and why of the paper's focus
    - a combination of the types listed above

4. Your readers will expect to see your **thesis** as the closing line of your introductory paragraph, which can be an effective way to transition from your introductory ideas to the main points of your paper. But the thesis does not have

to be the final line of the first paragraph. If you choose to place it elsewhere, be sure it is very clear to your readers which sentence is your thesis statement.

COMMON ERRORS:

- **Writing a "since the dawn of mankind" introduction.** Remember that your goal here is to intrigue and inspire, not diffuse. Always write something that you would be excited to read.

- **Composing an obligatory introduction.** If you are writing your introduction because you know it is required but your inspiration is minimal, consider how much less inspired your readers will be. Don't include an introductory paragraph just because you must; let it sing.

- **Including Wikipedia or another encyclopedia or dictionary definition in your introduction.** If you are looking for the authoritative voice of an effective definition, consider looking at disciplinary-specific source, such as a medical journal or a sociology textbook. Encyclopedias and dictionaries are not considered credible sources at the university level and beyond.

> "I believe that the ability to communicate complex ideas in a simple fashion is more important to engineering than technical ability. It helps you be sure you are solving the correct problem."
> *Andrew Gracey, Software Engineer*

EXERCISES:

Exercise 11.1

Consider at least five paragraphs you have written in the past week, whether for work, school, or personal use. Write the first line of each on the lines below. If you had been a member of your own audience, would you have chosen to read on? Why or why not? If not, what revisions would you make?

1.
2.
3.
4.
5.

Exercise 11.2

Consider a writing assignment you will need to undertake in the near future. How might you approach an introduction using each of the following approaches? Be specific as you answer.

1. A related story:
2. A provocative question or series of questions:
3. A hypothetical scenario:
4. A surprising fact or series of facts:
5. An engaging direct quotation:
6. A striking statement:
7. Background information or context:
8. An opposing argument:
9. The who, what, where, when, and why of the paper's focus:
10. A combination of the types listed above:

Exercise 11.3

Select one of the examples from either Exercise 10.3 or Exercise 11.2 and write an introduction. Once you have finished, ask yourself the following questions:

1. Have you included a catchy first line?
2. Which of the suggestions listed in Exercise 11.2 have you used to interest and inspire your readers?
3. Have you included a clear, concise thesis statement?
4. If you were a member of your own audience, would you keep reading? Why or why not?
5. What further revisions do you need to make?

CHAPTER 12.

BODY PARAGRAPHS

Every body paragraph must adhere to the simple math of topic sentence + evidence = paragraph. [Image: Alejandro Alvarez | Unsplash]

DEFINITION TO REMEMBER:

- **Topic Sentence + Evidence = Body Paragraph**

RULES TO REMEMBER:

1. Each body paragraph must adhere to the simple math of *topic sentence + evidence = paragraph*. Remember that your readers will expect a new topic with each new paragraph, or at least a very clear progression forward of ideas.
2. If it seems appropriate, include a *summary sentence* at the end of each body paragraph to remind your readers of your overall purpose for the essay.
3. While there is no rule about the expected length of a paragraph, your readers will expect general uniformity. If your opening paragraphs are short, maintain that pattern throughout your essay. If your opening paragraphs are long, all paragraphs in your essay should be similarly long.

> "I always imagine my emails being carefully read by a panel of experts critiquing me on my efforts years after I sent them. I put a lot of time into crafting well-articulated emails to ensure my point is coming across without being too rushed or too lengthy no matter who the audience. I never include anything I wouldn't want written on my tombstone." *Dale Harris, IT Professional*

COMMON ERRORS:

- **Forgetting to adhere to the simple math of the paragraph.** When we "just write," we tend to either contradict or repeat ourselves. While "just writing" is the preferred approach for a first draft, use the revision process to apply the simple math that will aid your readers in reading quickly, efficiently, and energetically.

- **Assuming that a topic sentence is not necessary with each new paragraph.** When you assume, your readers will assume, and those assumptions almost never align.
- **Losing track of your main purpose.** Here is where the umbrella metaphor can be helpful. Once you have a clear thesis statement, imagine each new body paragraph resting beneath that open umbrella. Does the new topic fit? Does it move your argument forward? Is your thesis statement broad enough to include all that you hope to include, and yet narrow enough to be manageable in the length required?

EXERCISES:

Exercise 12.1

Consider an essay or longer piece you have written in the past week, whether for work, school, or personal use. When you consider the body paragraphs of your essay, did you adhere to the following structure? If not, what revisions should you make?

1. Body Paragraph –
    - Topic sentence:
    - Evidence:

2. Body Paragraph –
    - Topic sentence:
    - Evidence:

3. Body Paragraph –

- Topic sentence:
- Evidence:

4. Body Paragraph –
   - Topic sentence:
   - Evidence:

5. Body Paragraph –
   - Topic sentence:
   - Evidence:

6. (+ additional as needed)

Exercise 12.2

A friend of yours has been asked by his supervisor to write an eight-page assessment of a team he serves on at work. The assignment is due tomorrow, but your friend has been unable to focus his ideas. What clear steps would you offer your friend so he is able to complete the task in an effective and timely manner? List your advice below as clearly and simply as possible:

1.
2.
3.
4.
5.

Exercise 12.3

Consider an essay or writing assignment you will need to complete in the next week, whether for school, work, or home. What is your topic? What is your claim about that topic? Complete the following to ensure that you will hold to the simple math of an effective body paragraph:

1. Body Paragraph –
   - Topic sentence:
   - Evidence:

2. Body Paragraph –
   - Topic sentence:
   - Evidence:

3. Body Paragraph –
   - Topic sentence:
   - Evidence:

4. Body Paragraph –
   - Topic sentence:
   - Evidence:

5. Body Paragraph –
   - Topic sentence:
   - Evidence:

6. (+ additional as needed)

CHAPTER 13.
CONCLUSIONS

For many readers, your concluding words are what they will remember long after they have finished reading your piece. For that reason, your concluding paragraph is critical. [Image: Vlad Shapochnikov | Unsplash]

DEFINITION TO REMEMBER:

- **Thesis + Wisdom + Catchy Last Line = Conclusion**

RULES TO REMEMBER:

1. Much as your introduction gives readers a first impression of who you are and what you hope to accomplish, your conclusion is your chance to offer final wisdom. For many readers, your concluding words are what they will remember long after they have finished reading your piece. For that reason, your concluding paragraph is critical.
2. Always end your essay in a way that reinforces your thesis and your purpose. A conclusion must provide a sense of closure. Readers should recognize your final paragraph as an ending. If you feel compelled to type the words "The End," you're not there yet.
3. Remember to look ahead. Is there future research that you intend or would recommend? Is there something specific you hope your readers will do with the ideas you have shared? Is there a new direction to turn? How can you use your conclusion to keep your readers thinking, even after they have set your essay aside?
4. Remind your readers of your overall **thesis**. Do not merely repeat your thesis. If you have added sufficient evidence in your essay to support your claim, your thesis should sound different to your readers than it did in the introduction. As you remind your readers of your purpose, allow your thesis to express the fullness of all of the evidence you have brought to bear.
5. Offer **wisdom** that your readers can take with them. Much like the introduction, here are several possible approaches for ending an essay well:

    - a related story
    - a provocative question or series of questions
    - a hypothetical scenario
    - a surprising fact or series of facts

- an engaging direct quotation
- a striking statement
- background information or context
- an opposing argument
- the who, what, where, when, and why of the paper's focus
- a combination of the types listed above

6. Finish with a **catchy last line** that is both conclusive-sounding and memorable. Much like a catchy first line, an effective last line should be concise, poetic, persuasive, and provocative.

COMMON ERRORS:

- **Tacking on a placeholder conclusion.** Writers are often fatigued by the time they are ready to write that final paragraph, and, unfortunately, it shows. As with any kind of writing, if you are finding the work tedious, imagine how uninterested your readers will be. Always save time to set your work aside and refresh before writing your conclusion; the added effort will always pay off.

> *"Writing well may offer little respect, but writing poorly certainly loses it."*
> *David Hartmann, Director of Client Success*

- **Repeating what has been said already.** While many of us were taught in elementary school to use the conclusion as an opportunity to remind your readers of everything you just said, an effective post-elementary school conclusion should aspire for more than merely repetition.

EXERCISES:

Exercise 13.1

Consider a writing assignment you will need to undertake in the near future. How might you approach a conclusion using each of the following approaches? Be specific as you answer.

1. A related story:
2. A provocative question or series of questions:
3. A hypothetical scenario:
4. A surprising fact or series of facts:
5. An engaging direct quotation:
6. A striking statement:
7. Background information or context:
8. An opposing argument:
9. The who, what, where, when, and why of the paper's focus:
10. A combination of the types listed above:

Exercise 13.2

Consider at least five paragraphs you have written in the past week, whether for work, school, or personal use. Write the last line of each on the lines below. If you had been a member of your own audience, would you have found the last line conclusive but memorable? Why or why not? If not, what revisions would you make?

1.
2.
3.
4.
5.

Exercise 13.3

Select one of the examples from Exercise 13.1 and write a conclusion. Once you have finished, ask yourself the following questions:

1. Which of the suggestions listed in Exercise 13.1 have you used to interest and inspire your readers? Why?
2. Have you included a repetition of your thesis statement that is a fuller, more complete version of the statement you included in your introduction?
3. Have you included a catchy last line?
4. If you were a member of your own audience, would you find the conclusion memorable? Why or why not?
5. What further revisions do you need to make?

PART IV.

THE PROCESS OF WRITING WELL

When I learned to write in my elementary school years, the teacher would give the class a prompt that my classmates and I then dutifully tried to answer. "Describe the life cycle of a monarch butterfly," for example, or "Write about your favorite summer memory." We are schooled from our earliest years that our purpose is to complete the assignment; the best writing reaches a broad, general audience, and our role as a writer is to keep out of the way as much as we are able to. But the kind of writing that is clear, effective, and meaningful does just the opposite: (1) our purpose is the claim we are making about the topic we have chosen, (2) our audience must be as specific as possible, and (3) we must have a solid sense of who we are as writer if we hope to communicate successfully. In addition, we should be able to name, understand, and articulate the medium we have chosen for communication to ensure that we are using that medium efficiently and appropriately.

CHAPTER 14.

PURPOSE

For many students, Aristotle's Rhetorical Triangle presenting the three modes of persuasion – logos, pathos, and egos – becomes lost in the trees of misremembered concepts. Our revised triangle applies Aristotle's ideas directly to today's modes of writing, demanding purpose, awareness, and intentionality every time we write. [Image: Arnaud Mesureur | Unsplash]

DEFINITION TO REMEMBER:

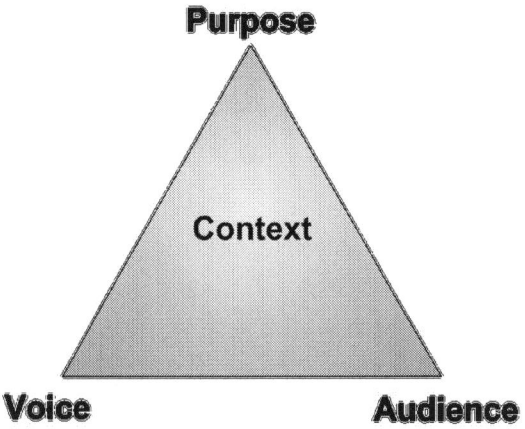

A 21st Century Rhetorical Triangle

RULES TO REMEMBER:

1. When we learn to write in our elementary years, we are given a prompt or question and asked to write:

   - *Describe your summer vacation.*
   - *Outline the life cycle of the butterfly.*
   - *Write a biography about someone famous in American history.*

   Our purpose is to satisfy the prompt and earn approval from our teacher. For many of us, that academic sense of purpose carries on into our high school and college years. Our purpose for writing comes externally from whomever has given us the assignment – a reliance that often leads to resentment when we have no interest in the purpose we have been given.

   But an external purpose will rarely lead to inspired writing. Our best writing comes when we have an internal **purpose**:

a reason to communicate that is inspired, energetic, and infectious.

2. Discovering purpose is your responsibility as a writer. No one wants to write about something distasteful or dull, but sometimes we are called to the challenge. When you are given a prompt, how will you locate a nugget of interest? What can you bring to the topic that is uniquely from you, your life, or your experiences? What additional research might help you discover something new and intriguing? What passions or future interests do you have that you might tie to the topic?

3. As you ponder purpose, consider the following questions:

   - When did you first notice or experience this issue?
   - What is the most challenging part of this issue?
   - What are some of the main causes of this issue?
   - Is there a situation or scene that is typical of this issue?
   - What do people stand to win or lose with regard to this issue?
   - Is what is at stake here inherently interesting to some people? Who are those people?

4. Only write what you would want to read. Consider the following prompt:

   - *Write a five-paragraph paper about the floor beneath your feet.* If this were your assignment for the next two hours, what would you do? What kind of essay would interest you as a reader? Even if you are in a room with dull brown carpet, here are some possibilities:
     - *a history of carpet manufacturing*
     - *an exploration of flammability and safety*
     - *the impact of color on a room*

- *a memory of a similar childhood carpet*
- *a story about grandparents who believed in brown*
- *an explanation of how to lay carpet*
- *an informational piece about who and how to hire carpet layers*
- *an essay about choosing carpet wisely*
- *an argument about carpets and allergies*
- *a list of curious facts about carpets in American homes*

Your purpose is up to you, regardless of how limiting a prompt may seem. Choose a direction that interests you, and find ways to connect with your topic so your purpose becomes internally driven rather than externally given.

5. Always prewrite. Prewriting comes in a variety of approaches, and it is up to you to discover what works best as you ponder a new idea. Keep in mind that prewriting does not have to mean sitting at a desk with your fingers on the keyboard. Some of the best prewriting happens when you are walking or driving or eating or taking a shower. Here are some options for effective prewriting as you discover your purpose:

- *brainstorming*
- *clustering / mindmapping*
- *freewriting*
- *journaling*
- *outlining*
- *question-asking*
- *looping*

Remember: Prewriting does not necessarily mean writing.

Some writers need to get their ideas down on paper or on a screen, while others prefer to mull ideas as they go about other tasks. Experiment with options until you discover what is most effective, efficient, and inspiring for you.

6. Ask yourself, *So what?* Why does your purpose matter? To whom does it matter? And does it really matter? Learn to ask yourself *So what?* continually and consistently throughout the writing process. The more often you ask, the less often your readers will feel the need to ask.

COMMON ERRORS:

- **Writing to a prompt without pondering a deeper sense of purpose.** When you are uninspired, your readers will be uninspired as well. Before you write, always take time to discover a reason for writing.

- **Blaming the prompt-giver for your own lack of interest.** The onus is on you to find your purpose, regardless of how uninspiring a prompt may be. Boring people are bored. What tools can you use to bring inspiration and energy to every new writing task?

- **Not taking the time necessary to prewrite and ponder.** Few of us can sit down cold to a writing prompt and produce excellent work. While we are sometimes called to do that, most situations allow a few days or hours before we need to begin writing. Use that time wisely.

> "I remind my children that regardless of any future personal and professional goals, always remain vigilant in the art and science of storytelling and story-writing. Your writing and grammar skills will improve, thereby presenting you as polished, sophisticated, and a benefit to your guild."
> *Patrick F. O'Neal,*
> *Pastor*

- **Neglecting to focus on a purpose that is broad enough to allow for discussion but narrow enough to be manageable.**

EXERCISES:

Exercise 14.1

Consider five writing tasks that you have completed recently, whether for school, work, or home. What was the purpose of each? Did you feel a personal connection to that purpose, or was it assigned to you? How might you have approached each task differently to ensure that your purpose was internal rather than external?

1.
2.
3.
4.
5.

Exercise 14.2

Consider the following topics. If you were asked to write a brief essay on each, what approach would you take that would interest you? How do you ensure that you write something you would enjoy to read, and that you effectively answer the question *So what?*

1. Politics
2. Baseball
3. Child-rearing
4. Part-time jobs
5. Recycling
6. Gardening

7. Space exploration
8. Capitalism
9. Religion
10. Education

Exercise 14.3

Consider a writing assignment that you will need to complete in the next week. What is the assignment, and why must you complete it? What will your purpose be in writing this assignment for your audience? Will this be something you would want to read? Why or why not? How will you effectively answer the question *So what*?

CHAPTER 15.

AUDIENCE

While an effective sense of purpose is critical, an understanding of your audience is just as important. Whether your goal is to impart information or to persuade someone to think differently about life, how can you expect success if you don't know to whom you are speaking? [Image: Stephan Wieser | Unsplash]

DEFINITION TO REMEMBER:

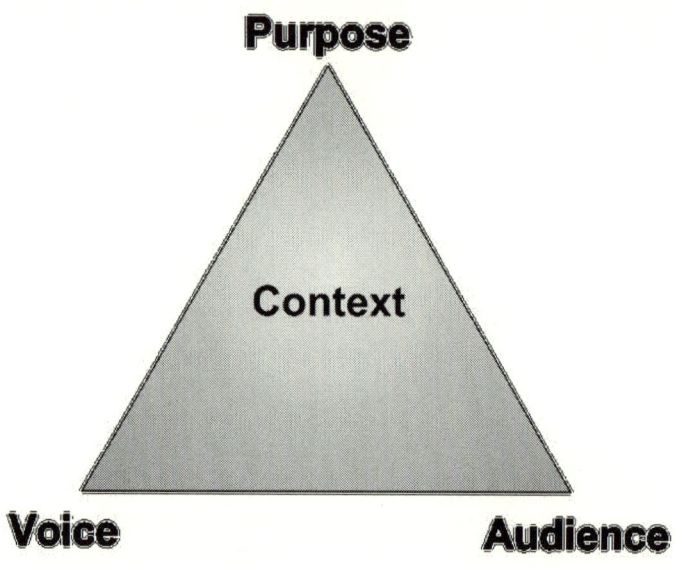

A 21st Century Rhetorical Triangle

RULES TO REMEMBER:

1. The Rhetorical Triangle is three-cornered to demonstrate that each of the three components is of equal importance. Most of us are taught that we should have a purpose when we write, but few of us are taught the importance of audience. When we are young, our audience is our teacher, which is

"As important as it is to have writing that is technically correct, your audience is more important. Codifying the importance of who and how has helped me in developing relationships." Byron Deming, Quality Assurance Analyst

likely why we are not taught to ponder a different, larger, or more complex audience. But take heed: While an effective sense of **purpose** is critical, an understanding of your **audience** is just as important. Whether your goal is to impart information or to persuade someone to think differently about life, how can you expect success if you don't know to whom you are speaking?

2. The first step is to identify your audience. As you ponder, consider the following:

   - Who, aside from you, has a stake in finding answers about this topic?
   - What do they have to lose or to gain from the issue?
   - Who has already written about or spoken about this issue?
   - Who would want to learn more about this issue? Why?
   - Who would disagree with you on this issue? Why? Write a single sentence in which you describe the audience you are considering.

3. The next step is to define your audience. The more specific your answers are and the narrower your audience is, the better you can tailor your writing to address your audience specifically and effectively. Consider the following questions:

   - What is the primary age group of your audience?
   - What is the primary gender?
   - What is your audience's race and/or cultural background?
   - Where is your audience located?
   - What is their education level and economic status?
   - What primary religious beliefs do they hold?

- What does your audience value? What are their interests?
- Are you addressing a specific group of people? For example, are you addressing coworkers, business executives, teachers, or liberals?

4. How much does your audience know about your topic?

    - How much background will you need to provide?
    - Are there specific terms or jargon that you will need to define, or will your audience have a familiarity with that language already?
    - What bias does your audience hold about your topic? What assumptions might they make, and how can you address those assumptions directly?
    - What other misconceptions might your audience have about the topic?

5. Keep in mind what will move your audience. Will the members respond best to emotion, logic, credible or famous sources, or a combination of the three?
6. Picture your audience as you prewrite, as you write, and as you revise. If you are writing to a single person, picture that person sitting across from you, listening as you read your ideas aloud. If you are writing to a convention center full of people, picture their sea of faces as they hear your words. At what point are they interested, angry, bored, curious, or emotional? What can you do to ensure that your approach is the most effective approach possible for the audience you plan to address?
7. How do you hope your audience will think differently about the world after reading your work? Has your tone achieved your purpose? Have you included sources that will interest and persuade your audience?

COMMON ERRORS:

- **Assuming that the instructor is the audience**, and neglecting to realize the importance of weighing who your audience is every time you write.
- **Arguing for a "general audience."** There is no such thing as a general audience. An audience can be exceptionally narrow or exceptionally broad, but there are always distinguishing factors. Take the time to answer the questions in item #2 above *every time you write*, and you may be surprised.
- **Neglecting to narrow your audience appropriately.** The narrower your audience is, the more effective and persuasive your writing will be. It is far easier to write to a group of 16 year olds than to a general age group spanning from 3 to 103. Some of the key factors to consider as you narrow, include: age, location, education, class, and career choice.
- **Forgetting to focus on the audience with every word, every fact, every claim, every source, and every story.** Too often we slide into a nonexistent or general audience; it takes work to keep ourselves focused on the audience we intend to reach.

EXERCISES:

Exercise 15.1

Consider five writing tasks that you have completed recently, whether for school, work, or home. What was the purpose of each? Who was your audience for each? Did you write with the audience keenly in mind? How might an intentional sense of audience have changed your approach to each of those writing tasks?

1.
2.

3.
4.
5.

Exercise 15.2

Select a writing task that you have completed recently or that you intend to complete, and answer the following questions:

1. Who, aside from you, has a stake in finding answers about this topic?
2. What do they have to lose or to gain from the issue?
3. Who has already written about or spoken about this issue?
4. Who would want to learn more about this issue? Why?
5. Who would disagree with you on this issue? Why?

Write a brief paragraph in which you describe the audience you are considering.

Exercise 15.3

This level of audience analysis should happen *every time you write*, whether you are writing a text, an email, a work document, or an academic essay. Consider a writing assignment that you will need to complete in the next week. What is the assignment, and what will your purpose be in writing this assignment for your audience? Write an Audience Description in which you describe your audience carefully and thoroughly. An effective Audience Description should be a brief but thoughtful paragraph that describes (1) who your audience is, using the questions in items #2 and #3 above for guidance;

(2) what approach you will use with that audience; and (3) how you will reach that audience (blog? email? pamphlet? website? publication? magazine? etc.).

CHAPTER 16.

VOICE

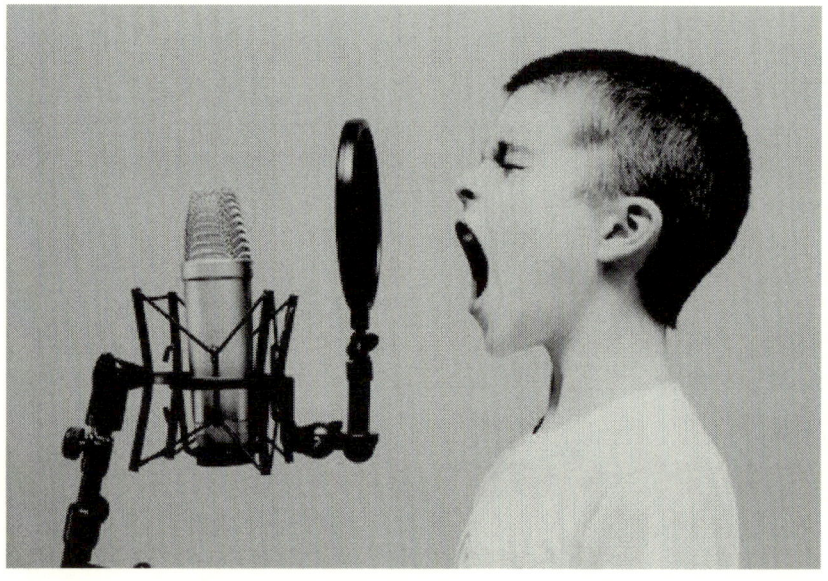

Be true to your strengths. The more authentic you are in your writing, the more likely your readers will be to listen to what you have to say. [Image: Jason Rosewell | Unsplash]

DEFINITION TO REMEMBER:

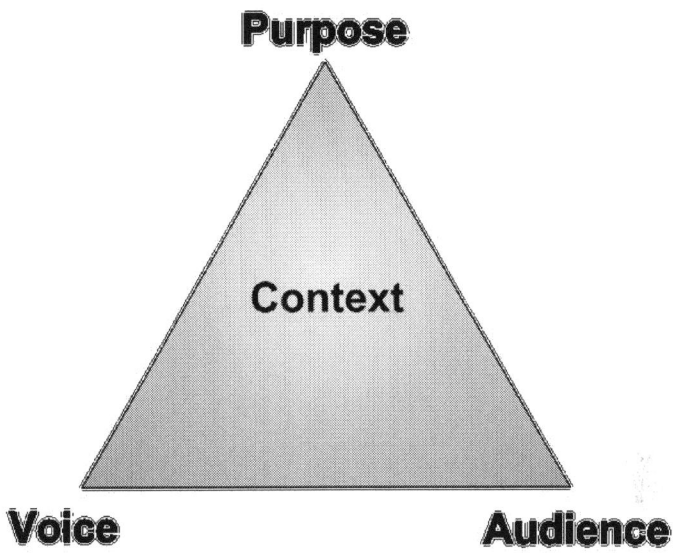

A 21st Century Rhetorical Triangle

RULES TO REMEMBER:

1. Who you are is just as critical as your purpose and your audience. Without a keen understanding of your own background, assumptions, and biases, you may say or express your ideas in a way that have an effect on your audience that you never intended. If, for example, you are a retired African-American man in your 70s who had an affluent career and home in the Pacific Northwest, you must be mindful of who you are when you speak to a group of young single white mothers in southern Louisiana or a community of Chinese-American high school students in northern California. Your voice can have a profound effect on how your audience hears the ideas you hope to convey.
2. Be honest with yourself. Are you able to define yourself

with the same specific terms that you defined your audience? Consider the following:

- How old are you?
- What is your gender?
- What is your race and/or cultural background?
- Where are you located, and where are you from?
- What is your education level and economic status?
- What primary religious beliefs do you hold?
- What do you value? What are your interests?
- Are you part of a specific group of people? What groups do you associate with, and how would other people classify you?
- What biases do you hold? What misconceptions might you have about a particular topic or group of people, particularly considering your answers to the questions above?
- What language or jargon do you use that others might not immediately understand? What terms will you need to define as you speak to others? What background information will you need to provide?

3. Be honest with your readers. Your audience will nearly always be in a hurry, looking for holes to poke in your argument and your character. If you exaggerate or inflate yourself in any way, your audience will likely set your ideas aside as inconsequential or silly. Instead be forthright and honest with your audience, seeking answers alongside them rather than setting out to prove your superiority. As always, only write the words that you would want to read, and most of us don't like to be talked down to, particularly if we suspect that someone is not being entirely honest with us.

4. Choose your words, examples, and approach mindfully. Your voice is uniquely yours and the best part of what you have to offer in this information-drenched world. The better you understand the elements that define who you are, the better you will be able to use your voice with intentionality. Consider the following as you seek to define your own voice. Are the choices you make intentional or be default? Are the habits you have effective in speaking to the audiences you intend to reach, or should you learn to be more nimble with the elements that comprise your narrative voice?

    - *word choice*
    - *sentence length*
    - *paragraph length*
    - *point of view*
    - *punctuation choices*
    - *emotional appeals*
    - *appeals to logic*
    - *storytelling*
    - *use of bullets, direct quotes, charts, or illustrations*
    - *humor*
    - *direct vs. indirect address*
    - *opposing arguments*
    - *conflict*
    - *authority*
    - *diction, syntax, and tone*

5. Be true to your strengths. Not everyone can master every element of effective rhetoric – nor should we. Instead learn

to articulate who you are and how you come across to others, and play up the areas where you feel most comfortable and inspired. For example, if humor comes naturally to you, find ways to incorporate it in your writing. If you appreciate a sad story, consider how to use emotional appeals and storytelling in your writing. The more authentic you are in your writing, the more likely your readers will be to listen to what you have to say.

COMMON ERRORS:

- **Assuming that voice comes naturally and therefore cannot be altered.** While your spoken voice is inherently you, how you express that voice in writing is dependent on a number of choices that can and should be made with intentionality.

> *"The tormented artist shtick is passé – I am into authentic. Write from who you are, where you are, and where you've actually been." Paul Ruddock, Doctor of Ministry Student*

- **Not realizing that voice is as important as purpose and audience.** We typically learn about purpose in elementary school, and – if we're lucky – we begin to consider audience in high school. A discussion of voice sometimes happens in late high school or college, but many writers never hear it at all, which is a shame. If purpose, audience, and voice are all equally important, how can you ensure that your approach to writing honors them all evenly and consistently?

- **Not recognizing the ways that voice can inspire or shut down an audience.** We have all watched the eyes of someone we are speaking to slowly glaze over with boredom, anger, or irritation, even when we are begging them to keep listening, but once that wall goes up, it can be difficult to get the other person listening well again. What can you do in your writing to ensure that the wall stays down and communication remains effective?

EXERCISES:

Exercise 16.1

Answer the following questions as thoughtfully and thoroughly as possible.

1. How old are you?
2. What is your gender?
3. What is your race and/or cultural background?
4. Where are you located, and where are you from?
5. What is your education level and economic status?
6. What primary religious beliefs do you hold?
7. What do you value? What are your interests?
8. Are you part of a specific group of people? What groups do you associate with, and how would other people classify you?
9. What biases do you hold? What misconceptions might you have about a particular topic or group of people, particularly considering your answers to the questions above?
10. What language or jargon do you use that others might not immediately understand? What terms will you need to define as you speak to others? What background information will you need to provide?

Exercise 16.2

Consider the following elements as you seek to define your own voice. How do you fare, and what would you like to improve or change?

1. word choice

2. sentence length
3. paragraph length
4. point of view
5. punctuation choices
6. emotional appeals
7. appeals to logic
8. storytelling
9. use of bullets, direct quotes, charts, or illustrations
10. humor
11. direct vs. indirect address
12. opposing arguments
13. conflict
14. authority
15. diction, syntax, and tone

Exercise 16.3

Consider a writing assignment you have completed recently, whether for work, school, or personal use. What was you purpose, and who was your audience? How would you describe your voice, using the language in the chapter above? Was your voice effective in achieving what you hoped to accomplish? Why or why not? If not, what revisions would you make?

CHAPTER 17.

CONTEXT

While the three points of the triangle – purpose, audience, and voice – are important in determining how your voice will be heard, where your voice will be heard can be equally important. [Image: Fabien Barral | Unsplash]

DEFINITION TO REMEMBER:

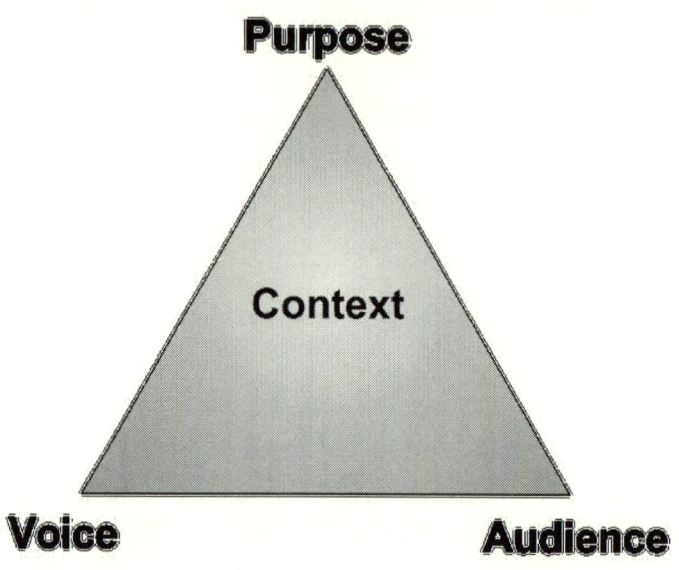

A 21st Century Rhetorical Triangle

RULES TO REMEMBER:

1. While the three points of the triangle – purpose, audience, and voice – are important in determining *how* your voice will be heard, *where* your voice will be heard can be equally important. Are you writing an academic essay, an online discussion forum, an email, an evaluation, a review, a blog, a post, an article, a letter, or a text?
   Will your words appear on printed paper or on a screen? If they will be printed, will they be on paper, in a book, on a pamphlet or informational guide, in a magazine or journal, or on the pages of a newspaper? If they will appear on a screen, are they more likely to appear on someone's desktop computer, laptop computer, iPad, TV, smart phone, smart watch, a large smart screen, or another device? How does the context affect how and what you will say?

2. Consider the visuals. How does the context affect the visuals that will either accompany or be incorporated in your work? Are short paragraphs and bulleted ideas preferable, or are longer paragraphs acceptable? Will there be pictures or graphics to augment your ideas, or do you need to spend more time offering specific images and details? Would break-out boxes make your ideas more readable, and how might that affect the flow of your ideas? As you consider the following options, weigh carefully whether their inclusion would benefit or detract from the influence of your words:

   - *colored fonts*
   - *varied point sizes*
   - *strategic white space*
   - *bulleted lists*
   - *pictures*
   - *graphs*
   - *charts*
   - *break-out boxes*
   - *live links*
   - *music*
   - *videos*
   - *slides*
   - *sound bites*
   - *interactive maps*
   - *questionnaires or surveys*
   - *pop-up images*
   - *mind-maps*

When you include visuals, the information should not repeat what is already in your text. Always be mindful of how the two come together to create a more complex and persuasive whole.

3. Consider your tone. The more masterful we are at using technology to communicate, the more adept we are becoming at **code shifting**. Even as we learn to subconsciously shift the tone of our writing, it will always behoove us to be intentional in order to ensure that we are as clear and persuasive as possible.

    For example, as you type an academic essay on your laptop while monitoring work emails on a desktop and occasionally checking social media on a smart phone, you shift your linguistic code with each new device and context. While you may not always need to remind yourself to monitor your tone as you move from a formal email to your boss to an emoji-based text to your spouse, you need to be careful not to slip between the two. Many of the components of voice apply here as well. How do each of these affect the impact you are hoping to have on your readers?

    - *word choice*
    - *sentence length*
    - *paragraph length*
    - *point of view*
    - *punctuation choices*
    - *emotional appeals*
    - *appeals to logic*
    - *storytelling*
    - *humor*
    - *direct vs. indirect address*

- *opposing arguments*
- *conflict*
- *authority*
- *diction, syntax, and tone*

COMMON ERRORS:

- **Assuming that *writing is just writing* without pondering the effects of varying contexts.** While the written medium has always had an impact on the message, today's constantly shifting contexts have an even greater effect. The more aware we are of the contexts we are sliding between, the more impactful our words will be.

> "Working with social media requires having an excellent ability to be quick and to the point while adhering to AP standards and maintaining a professional tone."
> *Jonathan Esterman, Billing & Collections Specialist*

- **Neglecting to consider the impact of visuals and live information on our writing.** While these additions do not always replace our words, they can alter the approach that we take. Keep a wide-angle view of your project: What is best heard? What is best seen? How can you communicate in ways that are memorable, intentional, and mindful of how and where your readers will receive your message?

- **Remaining inflexible in an era that demands flexibility.** While the simple math of effective writing remains stable, the means with which we share our writing with one another is continually changing. The more flexible we are in our efforts to reach others, the more likely we are to be heard.

EXERCISES:

Exercise 17.1

Consider five writing tasks that you have completed recently, whether for school, work, or home. What was the purpose of each? Who was your audience for each? What was the context for each? Consider a new context for each of the tasks you list below: If it was an essay, what if it had been a long email? If it was a report for work, what if it had been a social media blog? Consider the impact each shift in context would have on your final product.

1.
2.
3.
4.
5.

Exercise 17.2

Select one of the writing tasks from Exercise 17.1 above, and consider how you might incorporate the following additions. Would the item list add or detract from your argument? Why? How would you define each item in terms that would apply specifically to your topic?

1. Colored fonts and varied point sizes
2. Pictures
3. Graphs or Charts
4. Charts
5. Break-out boxes
6. Live links
7. Music
8. Videos

9. Interactive maps
10. Questionnaires or surveys

Exercise 17.3

Consider a writing assignment you intend to write in the near future, whether for work, school, or personal use. What is you purpose, and who is your audience? What context will you use and why? What impact will that context have on your final product? If you could choose a different context, what would you choose? Why?

CHAPTER 18.

CLAIMS AND APPEALS

We all know the person who offers unsolicited advice or repeats an opinion over and over without offering solid evidence. Don't be that person. Once you have stated your claim, move on to the evidence and appeals necessary to persuade your readers that your idea is worthy. [Image: Cortney Shegerian | Unsplash]

DEFINITION TO REMEMBER:

- **4 Claims = Fact, Value, Cause and Effect, Policies**
- **3 Appeals = Reason, Emotion, Character**

RULES TO REMEMBER:

1. Your thesis is a claim that must be debatable. Reasonable

claims typically fall into one of four categories: fact, value, cause and effect, and policy.

- **Claims of Fact** are logical claims that sound like facts but are not easily measured, which makes them debatable. When you make a claim of fact, be careful to include both sides of the argument to demonstrate why your claim is the most reasonable.

  - *Women are more effective multi-taskers than men.*
  - *Dogs are better listeners than cats.*
  - *The United States Postal Service will cease to exist in the next 10 years.*

- **Claims of Value** suggest a statement of value that typically requires an evaluative approach. When you make a claim of value, be sure you define your terms meticulously since your audience may not hold to the same values that you do.

  - *Wallace Stegner was the best Western American writer of his generation.*
  - *The Jeep Wrangler is an excellent car for value and durability.*
  - *The K-12 public school system is always a better choice than paying for private school.*

- **Claims of Cause and Effect** argue for a link between a cause and an effect that is not necessarily self-evident. Similarly to the value claim, a writer must define his or her terms carefully to ensure that the audience understands and agrees with the foundation of values.

  - *Kids who play team supports are harder-working employees when they reach adulthood.*

- *The introduction of the smart phone in 2007 has impeded the younger generation's ability to engage socially.*
- *Exposure to violent video games has led to an increasingly more violent American society.*

◦ **Claims of Policy** often occur alongside any of the previous three kinds of claims, suggesting a solution or policy change as a strategy for solving the problem that was introduced. A policy claim is an effective way to call your readers to action, although be sure to define clearly what steps you believe should occur in order for the new policy or solution to be put into place.

- *The punishment for drunk driving should be an automatic loss of license, jail time, and community service hours.*
- *All Protestant pastors should undergo emotional intelligence assessment before ordination.*
- *Airlines should be required to allow each passenger one checked suitcase and one carry-on bag free of charge.*

All of the above claims may be used individually or in combination.

2. As you support your claim and refute opposing arguments, your appeals will typically fall into one of three categories: reason, emotion, and character.

- **Appeals to Reason** include facts, evidence, surveys, and specific examples. In most cases, if an appeal to reason cannot be seen and measured, it will not be considered reasonable and, therefore, persuasive.
- **Appeals to Emotion** include stories and anecdotes that trigger an emotional response in a reader. While emotional appeals can sometimes seem manipulative or overused, they can be surprisingly effective even when

a readership presents as grounded in logic and postmodern skepticism. An example of an appeal to emotion might be a story about children playing a game of stick ball on the streets of a war-torn city.

- **Appeals to Character** rely on your ability to show your audience that you are a person of sound, moral judgment and solid reputation, and, therefore, your audience should believe the claims you have made. We are typically more likely to accept advice from people we know and trust, which is where this appeal can be effective. Even if your readers have never heard your name before, you can lead them to trust you by sounding confident and authoritative, offering solid evidence, and assuring them that you are a calm and well-reasoned person.

> "As a teacher, writing helps me to communicate with students' families. Maintaining a positive connection between home and school helps my students be more successful." *Katrina Jones, Science Teacher*

As with the claims listed above, appeals may be used in combination – and typically are. Dr. Martin Luther King Jr. was one of the most effective orators and persuasive writers of the 20th century, and his writings frequently engaged appeals to reason, appeals to emotion, and appeals to character all in the same piece.

COMMON ERRORS:

- **Ignoring the simple math of persuasion.** If your thesis is a debatable claim, both sides of the argument must have some merit. How will you rationally and effectively demonstrate to your readers that your claim is the worthy choice?

- **Hurrying to an end result without walking through the appropriate claims and appeals.** Just as the simple math of the sentence equation, paragraph equation, and essay equation is critical to clear and effective communication, the proper use of claims and appeals are essential for successful persuasion. Consider your audience, choose wisely, and write intentionally.

- **Repeating a claim increasingly, more vehemently, rather than offering solid evidence.** We all know a person who offers unsolicited advice or repeats an opinion over and over without offering solid evidence. Don't be that person. Once you have stated your claim, move on to the evidence and appeals necessary to persuade your readers that your idea is worthy.

EXERCISES:

Exercise 18.1

For each of the following topics, write a sample (1) claim of fact, (2) claim of value, (3) claim of cause and effect, and (4) claim of policy:

1. Health care
2. Term limits
3. Marijuana

Exercise 18.2

For each of the topics in Exercise 18.1, select one of the possible claims and consider how you would present an (1) appeal to reason, (2) appeal to emotion, and (3) appeal to character:

1. Health care
   - Claim:
   - Appeal:
2. Term limits
   - Claim:
   - Appeal:
3. Marijuana
   - Claim:
   - Appeal:

Exercise 18.3

Consider a writing assignment you intend to write in the near future, whether for work, school, or personal use. What is you purpose, and who is your audience? What claim(s) will you include? Why? What appeal(s) will you include? Why?

CHAPTER 19.

CLARITY AND COHESION

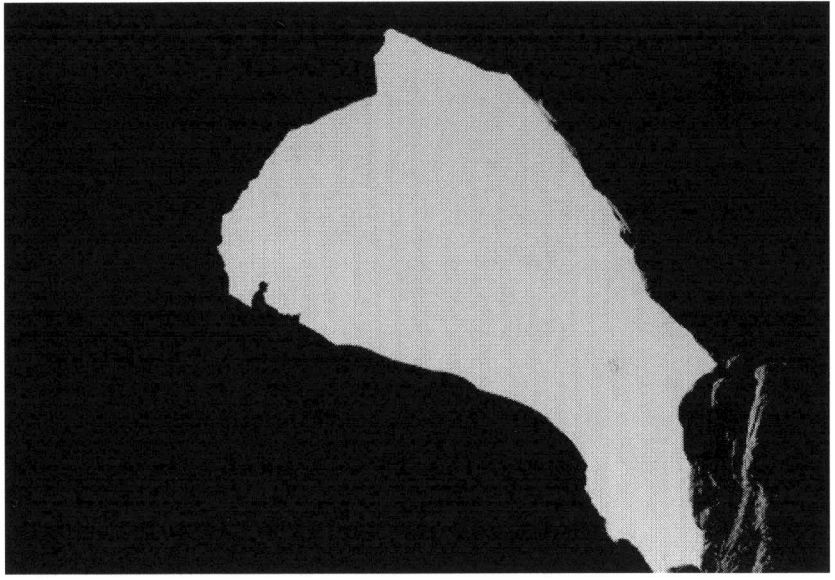

Clarity is achieved by holding to the simplicity of the mathematical equations, and cohesion comes when the thesis statement serves as an overarching umbrella holding all key ideas and evidence together. [Image: Jordan Webb | Unsplash]

DEFINITIONS TO REMEMBER:

- **Clarity = clear and easy to understand**

- **Cohesion = sticking together**

RULES TO REMEMBER:

1. **At the sentence level,** the words you use must be precise – and precisely appropriate for the audience you have chosen. Remember that too many words complicate matters. Instead of explaining yourself, select your words thoughtfully and precisely. Be sure, too, that your punctuation is correct and emphasizes the ideas that you want your audience to focus on. When in doubt, hold to the simple math: *subject + verb = sentence.*

   "Whether it is sermons, blog writing, or corresponding through emails, simple and concise writing is a crucial part of how I communicate. I'm always looking for skills to help me enhance my authentic writing voice." Nick Martineau, Senior Pastor

2. **At the paragraph level,** both clarity and cohesion are achieved when you follow the simple math of the paragraph: *topic sentence + evidence = paragraph.* Just as the thesis statement functions as an umbrella over the whole essay, consider the topic sentence as an umbrella over the individual paragraph.

3. **At the essay level,** the pattern is the same: Clarity is achieved by holding to the simplicity of the mathematical equations, and cohesion comes when the thesis statement serves as an overarching umbrella holding all key ideas and evidence together. Few writers achieve clarity and cohesion in a first draft, which is why revision is such a key part of the writing process. When you first sit down to write, allow yourself to simply write. When you sit down to revise,

apply the simple math of the sentence, paragraph, and essay; keep audience, purpose, and voice always at the forefront; and continually ask yourself *So what?*

COMMON ERRORS:

- **Over-explaining.** Too often we state our purpose once, then restate it again for clarity, and then restate it a third way to be sure our readers have understood what we intended to say. But what happens when we over-explain is our readers get lost in a mire of second-guessing and doubt. If you read an author's ideas once but still have questions, the best way to have those questions answered is to hear the evidence that is offered in support of the initial claim, rather than a continued restatement of the claim. Over-explaining is all-too-common – both on the internet and in the published world. The next time you find yourself irritated by the length of someone's communication, ask yourself whether it's an issue of over-explaining.

- **Over-thinking.** A sister error to over-explaining, over-thinking happens when we are not confident that our ideas are sound or our evidence is adequate. Instead of presenting what we have with authority, assured that the simple math will present our ideas with clarity and cohesion, we wonder about the countless other approaches we could have taken, muddling our initial ideas with insecure meanderings. When you revise, watch for over-explaining and over-editing; both will obfuscate your meaning and alienate your readers.

- **Under-editing.** As we will discuss in Chapter 20, revision is a critical stage of the writing process, and too often writers neglect to edit their work with a keen eye toward clarity and cohesion. When you edit, watch for the extraneous: words, punctuation, phrases, paragraphs, and ideas. Ask yourself if the paper would be weakened or strengthened by the absence.

We are often trained by teachers to believe that more is better, but it rarely is.

EXERCISES:

Exercise 19.1

The following paragraph contains sentences that interfere with its clarity and/or coherence. Read the paragraph aloud and consider (1) what elements are working well and (2) what elements need editing. Remember the simple math of *topic sentence + evidence (+optional summary sentence) = paragraph*.

I enjoy school because I am always eager to discover new sources and learn about new ideas. When I first walked into my Psychology 101 classroom, the professor opened with a discussion of the id, ego, and superego, and I was surprised to hear how many new ideas I could apply to my own understanding of the world around me. In my Archaeology 242 class, my professor told us she was visiting from a Navajo reservation in New Mexico, and it was fascinating to hear her discussions of skin walkers, pinon nuts, and hogans. As I walked to my English 210 class next, I was thrilled to see the leaves in the quad beginning to turn brilliant oranges and yellows. I stopped to feed a chipmunk the last bite of my bagel, and then I walked into Sturm Hall to meet my English professor. He lectured about books I had heard of but had never had time to read, and I left eager to find Siddhartha, The Little Red Pony, *and* Middlemarch. *And today was only Monday!*

Exercise 19.2

The following paragraph contains sentences that interfere with its clarity and/or coherence. Read the paragraph aloud and consider (1) what elements are working well and (2) what elements need editing. Remember the simple math of *topic sentence + evidence (+optional summary sentence) = paragraph*.

My nephew is an excellent baseball player. I attended his district tournament last weekend, and I was impressed to see him get a hit every time he was at bat. Once he even hit a line-drive past the third baseman for a triple that brought in two runners. The coach alternated my nephew between short stop and third base, and I counted six times that he caught infield pop flies for the out. In one play, the second baseman accidentally tripped a runner in the baseline, but the runner recovered and continued home. In the final inning, my nephew scooped up a grounder as it came off a bunt, tagged a runner headed for third base, and then threw hard and low to first for a second out. Right then, the wind whipped up from the south and we all had to dig sweatshirts out of our bags. My nephew's team placed second in the district tournament, thanks to several of my nephew's runs, and I look forward to watching them play at the state tournament next weekend.

Exercise 19.3

Consider a paragraph that you have written recently, whether for school, work, or home. Paste the paragraph here and read it with the same critical eye you used for Exercise 19.1 and Exercise 19.2. Underline your topic sentence, and weigh each subsequent sentence. Do you over-explain or over-think any of your ideas? Is your language clear and straight-forward? Do you adhere to the simple math of the sentence and the paragraph? Are your ideas cohesive, falling neatly beneath a clear topic sentence? What revisions do you need to make, if any?

ANSWER KEY:

Answer Key Exercise 19.1

I enjoy school because I am always eager to discover new sources and learn about new ideas. When I first walked into my Psychology 101 classroom, the professor opened with a discussion of the id, ego, and superego, and I was surprised to hear how many new ideas I could apply to my own understanding of the world around me. In my Archaeology 242 class, my professor told us she was visiting from a Navajo reservation in New Mexico, and it was fascinating to hear her discussions of skin walkers, pinon nuts, and hogans. ~~As I walked to my English 210 class next, I was thrilled to see the leaves in the quad beginning to turn brilliant oranges and yellows. I stopped to feed a chipmunk the last bite of my bagel, and then I walked into Sturm Hall to meet~~ My English professor ~~He~~ lectured about books I had heard of but had never had time to read, and I left eager to find Siddhartha, The Little Red Pony, and Middlemarch. And today was only Monday!

Answer Key Exercise 19.2

The following paragraph contains sentences that interfere with its clarity and/or coherence. Read the paragraph aloud and consider (1) what elements are working well and (2) what elements need editing. Remember the simple math of *topic sentence + evidence (+optional summary sentence) = paragraph.*

My nephew is an excellent baseball player. I attended his district tournament last weekend, and I was impressed to see him get a hit every time he was at bat. Once he even hit a line-drive past the third baseman for a triple that brought in two runners. The coach alternated my nephew between short stop and third base, and I counted six times that he caught infield pop flies for the out. ~~In one play, the second baseman accidentally tripped a runner in the baseline, but the runner recovered and continued home.~~ In the final inning, my nephew scooped up a grounder as it came off a bunt, tagged a runner headed for third base, and then threw hard and low to first for a second out. ~~Right then, the wind whipped up from the south and we all had to dig sweatshirts out of our bags.~~ My nephew's team placed second in the district tournament, thanks to several of my nephew's runs, and I look forward to watching them play at the state tournament next weekend.

CHAPTER 20.

REVISION AND CREATIVITY

Once the simple math is in place, be creative. The point of structure is not to lock you in, but to assure clarity and proper communication so that you may feel free to be creative with your details, your voice, and your ideas. [Image: James Zwadlo | Unsplash]

DEFINITION TO REMEMBER:

- **Revision = Content → Mechanics → Formatting**

RULES TO REMEMBER:

1. Revision is a three-step process:

    - **Content** – First read your work to gauge whether your content is as effective as it should be. Is your introduction clear and engaging? Is your thesis statement broad yet focused enough to be manageable? Do your body paragraphs each contain a clear topic sentence that falls neatly beneath your thesis? Is your evidence specific, applicable, and memorable? Is your conclusion persuasive and final-sounding? Are there places where your language could be more clear and cohesive? Is your purpose focused, your audience clear, and your voice intentional?

    - **Mechanics** – Once you are confident that your content is sound, read your work for mechanics, watching for errors in word choice, punctuation, structure, etc. If you see a content error as you are reading, pause in your step two of the revision process and take yourself back to step one until you are content that your work is done. Be wary of muddling these three varying steps, as writers who muddle them typically never complete them adequately.

    - **Formatting** – For this final step, select a formatting style that is required by your instructor or appropriate to your purpose, audience, and context. As you edit for proper formatting, watch for consistency, and be sure to look up any citation requirements that you are unsure about. If you are following an academic formatting style like APA, Turabian, or MLA, the requirements are precise.

2. While you might revise your work in this order – *Content* → *Mechanics* → *Formatting* – keep in mind that your readers will likely judge you in the opposite order: *Formatting* → *Mechanics* → *Content*. How can you ensure that your

formatting and mechanics are nearly error-free, ensuring that your readers will get to your content and still have confidence in your authority as a writer?
3. Once the simple math is in place, **be creative**. The purpose of the revision process is twofold: One purpose is to afford you time to ensure that you are aligned with the simple math of effective writing: at the sentence level, at the paragraph level, and at the essay level. The second purpose, once you are assured that the simple math is in place, is to allow you to be creative. The point of structure is not to lock you in, but to assure clarity and proper communication so that you may feel free to be creative with your details, your voice, and your ideas.
4. If you are writing an academic essay or an article for publication, don't forget the important of a good **title**. For many readers, the title is the first thing they see, which means they will sometimes decide whether or not to continue reading based on the title. Be sure yours is creative, enticing, and accurate.

   Consider the following examples. Would you keep reading? Why or why not?

   - *A Tough Lesson to Learn*
   - *Essay 3: The Visit*
   - *Discipline Issues: Absenteeism*
   - *The Man Who Turned into a Stick*
   - *A Small Incident*
   - *The Happy Man*
   - *The Lemon Trees*
   - *The First Long-Range Artillery Shell in Leningrad*
   - *Berry Picking*
   - *The Summer My Grandmother Was Supposed to Die*

COMMON ERRORS:

- **Skipping revision.** Many writers neglect to save time for this critical step in the writing process. Always, always allow proper time to read through and critique your own work in the three-step process outlined above. Accomplished writers will tell you that the most challenging part of writing comes in the revision; if you are simply writing a rough draft and calling it good, you are hardly writing at all.

- **Limiting the creativity.** While the simple math structure is the best way to ensure clarity and consistency in your work, it is not the ending point. Remember that the information age has virtually erased our need for informative pieces: Why would we need an explanatory essay when most of us can ask a smart watch or an in-home portable speaker? Therefore, your ability to add your own unique voice and perspective to the conversation is far more important than ever before. How will you ensure that your voice is authentically you and uniquely memorable?

- **Forgetting the title.** Whether you are writing an essay, an email, or a blog, titles are increasingly more important. How can you ensure that your readers find your title intriguing

> "I have always been longwinded in my writing but learned the trick of stepping away before submitting something final. When I am finished typing an email, I move onto something new before returning for one last proofread. I often find words or phrases that can be removed to create a more clear and concise message."
> *Meghan Gifford, Undergraduate Admissions Counselor*

enough to want to read your ideas? What kinds of titles are both engaging and revealing, mysterious and accurate?

EXERCISES:

Exercise 20.1

Select a writing task that you have completed recently, whether for school, work, or home. Walk it through the three-step revision process outlined above, and take notes on how your paper fares with each of the three steps. What changes do you need to make, and why? How does it help to separate the revision process into three individual steps?

1. Content
2. Mechanics
3. Formatting

Exercise 20.2

Consider five writing tasks that you have completed recently, whether for school, work, or home. How does your creativity show in each of these writing tasks? How might a reader know that each was written by you rather than another person of similar age, background, and intentions? What do you bring to your writing that is unique and memorable?

1.
2.
3.
4.
5.

Exercise 20.3

Track down at least 10 writing tasks that you have completed recently that required some kind of title – whether an essay or an email or something similar. List the titles that you chose on the lines below. Consider each title with the same critical eye as you considered the list of titles above. If you were reading your own ideas and spotted the title at hand, would you read on? Why or why not?

1.
2.
3.
4.
5.
6.
7.
8.
9.
10.

PART V.

RESEARCH

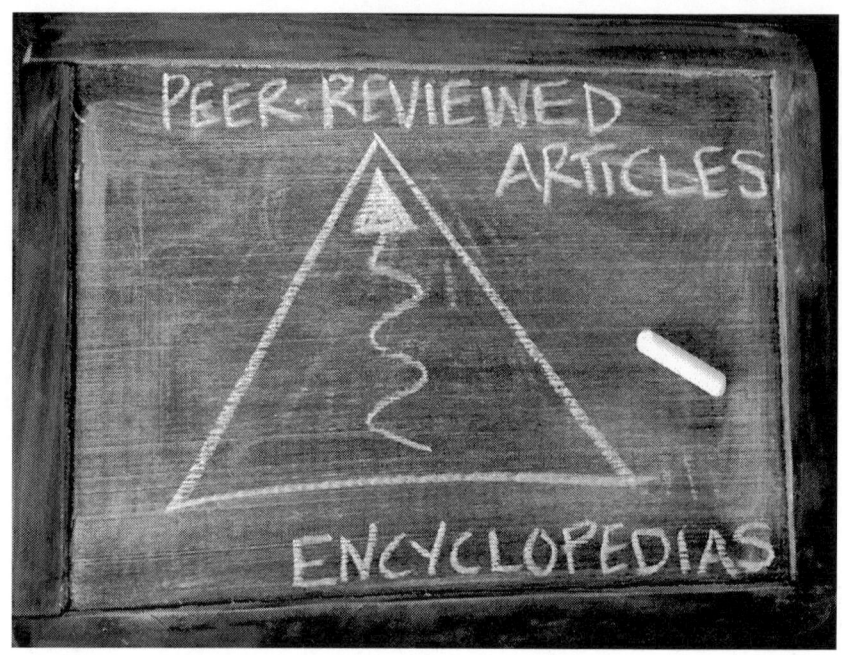

When I was assigned to research osmosis for my third-grade class in the 1970s, I walked to the science shelf in our elementary school library and gathered 9 or 10 books that boasted the most colorful pictures. When I wrote a university-level thesis on the AIDS epidemic in the 1980s, I visited several research libraries to collect armloads of books and academic journals to support my claim. The pre-web research field was narrow in comparison to the splendor of the internet, but at least we were assured that skilled reference librarians had vetted the materials we found. The credibility of your sources can determine the success of your claim, and in today's world, the task of determining credibility has grown steadily more daunting. How do you determine whether the information you find was gathered by experts or imagined by preteens? How do you decide whether to move ahead with evidence that sounds reasonable or discard it for fear of losing the trust of your audience?

CHAPTER 21.

FINDING CREDIBLE EVIDENCE

When you grab the first sources you can find, whether for an academic essay or a report at work, your readers will know immediately that you are not invested enough in your own ideas to seek out other worthy voices. And if you are not invested, why should they be? [Image: Glen Noble | Unsplash]

DEFINITION TO REMEMBER:

- **Credible = Trustworthy**

RULES TO REMEMBER:

1. Writers are now their own gatekeepers. Before the internet, reference librarians were our information gatekeepers. We trusted them to vet the worthy sources so we could confidently peruse library shelves and know that the items there were already pre-approved by a trained authority. Now that our access to information is boundless, the gatekeeping function falls to us. As a writer, the onus is on you to select sources that are trustworthy and reliable. The danger of choosing sources quickly and mindlessly is that you will lose your readers' trust. If you are looking for a good restaurant for a special evening out, do you ask the first people you spot or do you seek out the advice of trusted friends or restaurant reviewers? When you grab the first sources you can find, whether for an academic essay or a report at work, your readers will know immediately that you are not invested enough in your own ideas to seek out other worthy voices. And if you are not invested, why should they be? Here are some factors to consider as you determine whether a source is credible:

> *"Writing curriculum and faculty guides for a university psychology program connects me to the value of good academic writing. Shaping the minds and hearts of future counselors multiplies that value." Dave Beach, Special Appointment Faculty – Social Sciences*

- **Consider the author**. Is there an author listed? If so, who is it? Are you able to research the author further? If not, why not? Is it possible that no one is willing to stand behind the information, which is why you don't see a name attached? The absence of an author is not a reason to automatically discard a source, but it is a reason to proceed cautiously.

- **Check the date**. Is the information current? Has the website been updated recently? Some topics demand information that has been updated within the past hour – a work report, for example. Other topics rely on information from years past – an essay exploring the social life of Lord Byron, for example. But all web information should be monitored regularly if it is a reliable source. If you don't see a date, find a new source.

- **Look at the domain address**. Domains that are considered credible include .edu, which is reserved for colleges and universities, and .gov, which is used for government websites. Be wary of domains such as .com, .org, and .net, as they can be purchased and used by any individual for any purpose. The domain .org typically designates a non-profit organization, which means the source will likely have an agenda that you should be aware of. Sources do not have to be objective and non-biased in order for you to include them, but you do need to demonstrate to your readers an awareness of the motivations behind the sources you have selected.

- **Watch for a bibliography**. Reliable websites will include a list of sources for the information presented. Wikipedia and other open encyclopedias are not considered credible sources to include in an academic essay, for example, but they can be a helpful first stop when you learn to use the bibliography at the bottom of each entry to seek out new sources.

- **Critique the writing.** Do you see mechanical errors, inappropriate language, or odd tangents? A trustworthy source will have multiple checkpoints in place to ensure that the information presented is clear and error-free. If you see notable errors, find a new source.

- **Consider the site design.** Is the website professional, accessible, and easy to navigate? If not, why not? Credible sources will typically take great care to present their information in a professional manner. Don't waste your time with sources that do not appear clean, clearly written, and industry-approved.

2. Peer-reviewed sources carry the most authority, particularly in the academic world. A peer-reviewed article has been vetted, critiqued, and likely molded by peers who have years of experience in the subject matter at hand. While an article written for a popular magazine may be reviewed by an editor and a copy editor prior to publication, a peer-reviewed article is typically reviewed by a team of experts over many months and sometimes years.Here is a hierarchy of sources you might include, with the most authoritative and credible listed at the top:

Peer-reviewed academic journals

↓

Scholarly books

↓

Government sources

↓

Specialized trade books

↓

Specialized encyclopedias and dictionaries

↓

Specialized magazines

↓

Popular magazines, books, and articles

↓

General encyclopedias and dictionaries

If you aren't sure whether a source has been peer-reviewed, contact a reference librarian at your local university or public library. They are trained in navigating the complexities of credibly source gathering and are typically happy to help you evaluate quality as you peruse the internet.

3. When in doubt, consider your purpose and your audience as you weigh the credibility and worthiness of various sources. Does the source fit your purpose? Would your audience find the source believable, persuasive, and interesting, or would they be suspicious? Outside sources should strengthen your argument, not weaken it, so be particular in what you choose to include.

COMMON ERRORS:

- **Trusting the internet.** Rather than believing that what you find on the internet is true, what if you were to assume that any news feed or meme or authoritative source is actually the creation of a 14 year old in her pajamas in her bedroom with much too much time on her hands? How will you learn to use the gatekeeper checkpoints above to habitually vet all new information you encounter?

- **Choosing too quickly.** When we are in a hurry, it's tempting to do a surface search and assume that the first information we find is the best. But that is rarely the case. Take the time to critique your sources and follow links until you are confident that what you have is the most reliable information you can find.
- **Forgetting your audience.** Remember that you are not writing for yourself. Always keep your audience at the forefront of your mind. If they are sitting across from you, listening to your justification of why a particular source is worth listening to, how will they respond? Will they be inspired and persuaded, or merely tolerant and half-bored? How will you ensure that the sources you select make your argument far more powerful than if you had made your claim on your own without bringing in outside voices to join you?

EXERCISES:

Exercise 21.1

Find two credible sources for each of the topics listed below. How did you find each source? What makes it credible?

1. Making a career choice
2. Defining family
3. An act of heroism
4. A brush with death
5. The power of wealth

Exercise 21.2

Select a topic you have written about in the past or intend to write about in the near future. Make a cursory list of 10 possible sources for your topic. Using the language above, discuss the validity of each source and whether or not you would choose to include it in your piece.

1. Source:
2. Source:
3. Source:
4. Source:
5. Source:
6. Source:
7. Source:
8. Source:
9. Source:
10. Source:

Exercise 21.3

Consider a writing assignment you will need to undertake in the near future. Compile an Annotated Working Bibliography of at least 10 potential sources that you intend to use. List each source in the formatting style appropriate to your assignment, and follow each listing with a one- to two-sentence annotation in which you discuss why the source is credible and how it relates to your topic.

1. Source:
2. Source:
3. Source:
4. Source:
5. Source:

6. Source:
7. Source:
8. Source:
9. Source:
10. Source:

CHAPTER 22.
INCLUDING OUTSIDE EVIDENCE

Always demonstrate to readers why you are including a particular source. If you are presenting your topic from a podium and someone suddenly walks up beside you, clearly ready to take over the podium for a moment, wouldn't you explain to those gathered why that person is there and why you believe it is important to let him or her speak? [Image: Mike Wilson | Unsplash]

DEFINITION TO REMEMBER:

- **3 ways to include sources: (1) Summary, (2) Paraphrase, (3) Direct Quote**

RULES TO REMEMBER:

1. Always demonstrate to readers why you are including a particular source. If you are presenting your topic from a podium and someone suddenly walks up beside you, clearly ready to take over the podium for a moment, wouldn't you explain to those gathered why that person is there and why you believe it is important to let him or her speak? In a summary or paraphrase situation, the person will stand next to you while you share with your audience what you believe is important about that person's ideas. When you include a direct quote, you will step aside from the podium for a moment and allow the person to speak in your stead.

   Be careful, too, of allowing a list of outside speakers without commenting on why they are there or what you think of their ideas. Remember that the podium is yours and your readers expect to hear you speaking. If you opt to offer the microphone to someone else, always explain why.

2. A **summary** is when you include a shortened version of the source's ideas, allowing your readers a quick glimpse into the research you have done and its relevance to your topic. The summary is the most effective of the three kinds of source inclusion, as you can move quickly through a variety of sources. A summary is always shorter than the original source, and the following components must be included:

   - Author tag or source
   - Proper parenthetical or footnote.

Take care to use your own language and not the source's. If you find yourself repeating the sentence structure from the source or specific words, consider using a direct quote instead of summarizing.

3. A **paraphrase** is when you rewrite a source's ideas in your own words without necessarily offering a shorter version. In other words, if you were paraphrasing a single sentence from a source, you would include a single sentence in your own words (as opposed to a summary, which always shortens the original text). As with a summary, be careful to use your own words and not the source's. An effective technique is to read the material you intend to paraphrase and then set it aside for a time, allowing the words to sink in before you explain to your readers the content of the source. The following components must be included with a paraphrase as well:

    - Author tag or source
    - Proper parenthetical or footnote.

    The format of the parenthetical or footnote depends on the style you are required to use. Keep in mind that academic formatting styles are precise; when in doubt, look it up in the appropriate style guide.

4. A **direct quote** should be used only when the author's words are so eloquent or unique that it would not be appropriate to summarize what he or she has said. Do not include direct quotes merely to lengthen your essay. Consider your audience: Will they want to read the words directly from the source, or would it suffice to offer the ideas in your own words? Do not use a direct quote for statements of fact, numbers, or dates. As with a paraphrase or summary, the following components must be included with a direct quote:

    - Author tag or source

- Proper parenthetical or footnote.

Check the requirements of the formatting style you are using to determine whether a partial quote, full quote, or block quote is more appropriate. The punctuation is different for each situation, so be sure to double-check the style guide before you submit.

COMMON ERRORS:

- **Not including the proper components to lead a reader to the source information on your references page and to justify why you have elected to include a particular source.** In all formatting styles, you must include the author's last name and a page number, if you have one. Some formatting styles also include the publication date.

> "Being successful in event management is so much more than just verbally communicating with the people on your team, as there are many pieces to the puzzle when creating a productive event. Knowing how to communicate the procedures and processes in writing for your team and for your clients is a skill that takes time and practice, but is one of the most useful traits in the realm of event management."
> *Hannah Belleque, University Events & Facilities Coordinator*

- **Neglecting to make it clear to your reader when you are speaking and when your source is speaking.** Remember the podium image. If you are the one whom your audience expects to stand at the podium and speak, how will you make it clear to your readers when you are introducing a new voice, why you are introducing a new voice, and how that person will be permitted to join the conversation? How will you make it clear to your readers when it is you speaking again?

- **Not making intentional decisions about which kind of source inclusion will serve your audience best: summary, paraphrase, or direct quote.** Keep in mind that the most effective means of source inclusion is the summary and the most cumbersome is the direct quote. Many writers default to direct quotes because they believe that is the preferred approach, but that is not the case. Keep your purpose and audience in mind as you make intentional decisions about how to include the sources you have selected, and always ask yourself how your audience will respond to the decisions you make.

EXERCISES:

Exercise 22.1

Consider a writing assignment you will need to undertake in the near future. Find a credible source for the assignment that has at least one full page or longer of useful text. Write two or three sentences in which you adequately introduce and summarize the source, using the components discussed in this chapter.

Exercise 22.2

Consider a writing assignment you will need to undertake in the near future. Find a credible source for the assignment that has at least one full page or longer of useful text (select a different source from the one used in Exercise 22.1). Write two or three sentences in which you adequately introduce and paraphrase a brief selection from the source, using the components discussed in this chapter.

Exercise 22.3

Consider a writing assignment you will need to undertake in the near future. Find a credible source for the assignment that has at least one full page or longer of useful text (select a different source from the one used in Exercise 22.1 and Exercise 22.2). Write two or three sentences in which you adequately introduce and include a direct quote from the source, using the components discussed in this chapter.

PART VI.
_____

ACADEMIC FORMATTING
_____

In academic writing, the structure of a systematic format allows scholars to focus on content with an understanding that necessary components – publication dates, page numbers, citations, etc. – will always be in the same location. For students, these requirements often seem overly particular and unnecessary, but the craft of learning a format can be an effective precursor to writing in the work world. Even though you may never use APA formatting again once you earn your diploma, your chosen field likely has expectations and accepted best practices if you hope to be fully heard. The most common scholarly formats include APA style (from the American Psychological Association), MLA (from the Modern Language Association), and Turabian style (from the University of Chicago).

CHAPTER 23.

APA

DEFINITION TO REMEMBER:

- **APA = American Psychological Association** (typically used for social sciences)

RULES TO REMEMBER:

1. Use 12 point, Times New Roman font, with 1" margins on all sides.
2. Include a running head at the top of every page, with page number flush right. The running head itself is a shortened version of your paper's title, 50 characters or shorter.
3. Your essay includes 4 main sections: title page, abstract, body, and references. An abstract is required only on essays that are 8 pages in length or longer, and should be between 150 and 250 words.

SAMPLE PAPER:

Sample Paper in text-based format https://goo.gl/sBBj6j

DMIN726 Academic Essay: From Missional to Meaningful

Dr. Jennie A. Harrop

George Fox University

Abstract

Recent decades have affirmed that a missional approach is necessary if we are to move actively forward with the Great Commission. And while we have discussed home churches and missional involvement in the community, we have not acknowledged that the vernacular Tim Keller calls us to is nearly impossible to achieve in a culture that is deeply entrenched with biblical mythologies. In other words, how do we speak without raising walls of assumption, judgment, defensiveness, hurt, or anger? And, more importantly, how do we assess the assumptions, judgments, defensiveness, hurt, or anger of others if we cannot identify our own? Where are theologians and Christian leaders in the exploration of "Emotional Intelligence" or "Emotional Quotient" (EQ) popularized in Daniel Goleman's 1995 book *Emotional Intelligence?* How do we draw parallels between the tenets of EQ and the characteristics of Jesus Christ, and how do we ensure that our leaders embody those characteristics?

APA Essay Page 2

DMIN726 Academic Essay: From Missional to Meaningful

In his 2010 book *Nudge: Awakening Each Other to the God Who's Already There*, Leonard Sweet argues for a new kind of evangelism:

> The church has been more prone to "take a stand" on issues or "take a vote" on programs than touch. Touch is a centripetal force that includes and embraces. Taking stands is a centrifugal force that separates and divides. While the rest of the world is moving, the one taking a stand is frozen in time like kids playing freeze tag, waiting for the sign that says it's okay to move again. Christ ran around touching people and tagging them. Every Jesus tag offered freedom. Every Jesus tag let the person tagged know they had been touched by God. (p. 242)

The Pharisees operated by centrifugal force; Jesus perpetuates a centripetal force. As a church, we know this, and yet our efforts to stand for truth in the twenty-first century invariably repel rather than attract. According to Dan Kimball (2007), we are at a point where we need to offer both an apology and an apologetic: "While we need to stand strong on what we believe and need not be ashamed of the gospel in any way, we need to make sure we are presenting a biblical picture of the church and not perpetuating negative stereotypes. We need to offer an apologetic to correct misperceptions" (p. 250). The earliest roots of the missional movement, which has been a direct attempt to rescript our ecclesiastical centrifugal spin into an inclusive centripetal force, began with conversations in the early twentieth century about missionary methods that were deemed too reliant on western superiority (Aniol, 2016). As this healthy look at missionary ecclesiology spread, writers/theologians such as Darrell Guder, Ed Stetzer, Tim Keller, and Alan Hirsch carried the conversation into a broader church context in the late twentieth century, calling for a missional church. And while I agree with the end goal of the missional approach, I

APA Essay Page 3

believe the movement will eventually fade away without a direct and intentional articulation of (1) emotional quotient (EQ) and (2) audience quotient (AQ).

As Sweet (2014) argues in *Me and We: God's New Social Gospel*, the world's structural problems will remain as long as the individual human heart is ailing: "The [social gospel] movement's demise has been the subject of vast speculation and scrutiny, but it can be seen perhaps best this way: social gospelers tried to save an ailing turtle by switching out its shell, one embossed with the name 'Christianity'" (p. 3). The missional movement is in danger of a similar end. If we don't pause in our discussion of the core ideas of missiology to consider how individual hearts can be strengthened and encouraged, missional ideas will never rise from rhetoric to reality. According to Gillian Tett (2015), understanding the "messy gaps between rhetoric and reality" is critical: "Life does not always fit into the official descriptions of what people are *supposed* to do. Much of the time we ignore these messy realities" (p. 224). How, then, do we ensure that our discussion of missional church adequately prepares, equips, and strengthens the hearts of those who are sent to disciple? Are we embarking on missions – both around the globe and across the street – without properly training disciples? Peter Scazzero (2006) writes that a healthy understanding of self is essential: "The vast majority of us go to our graves without knowing who we are. We unconsciously live someone else's life, or at least someone else's expectations for us. This does violence to ourselves, our relationship with God, and ultimately others" (p. 66). In an effort to extend the missional conversation and keep the movement alive, an examination of individual EQ and AQ is an essential next step.

A Scriptural Shift

The scriptural underpinnings of the missional movement rest primarily in the Great Commission: "Then Jesus came to [the disciples] and said, 'All authority in heaven and on earth has been given to me. Therefore go and make disciples of all nations, baptizing them in the name of the Father and of the Son and of the Holy Spirit, and teaching them to obey everything I have commanded you. And surely I am with you always, to the very end of the age'" (Matt. 28:18-20 New International Version). But two problems are confronting us as we try to live into Jesus' commissioning: (1) We don't fully believe in our own authority and ability to do what Jesus is asking of us, and (2) We don't understand how to effectively speak to "all nations." In other words, while our godly purpose may make sense to us intellectually, we aren't properly equipped to live into it. As Mark Galli (2006) argues in *Jesus Mean and Wild: The Unexpected Love of an Untamable God*, when we begin to rationalize Jesus, we render the Great Commission vacuous and ineffective:

> We avoid the reality of Christ's power in a number of ways. For instance, we're tempted to spiritualize his power, to reduce the elemental potency and energy to a moment of personal religious inspiration. The stilling of the storm is about psychological storms in our lives. The healing of the lame is about solving emotional problems that cripple us. Jesus bringing sight to the blind is about God's ability to help us see our lives clearly. And so on and so forth. If we do that enough, we begin to think the Gospel stories are nothing but metaphors, and metaphors primarily about us." (p. 113)

How do we rescue Jesus' meaning "from the barnacles that have attached themselves to it over the centuries"? (Bailey, 2008, p. 343).

APA Essay Page 5

References

Aniol, R. (2011, October 12). A brief history of the missional church movement. *Religious Affections Ministries*. Retrieved from http://religiousaffections.org/articles/articles-on-church/a-brief-history-of-the-missional-church-movement/

Bailey, K. E. (2008). *Jesus through Middle Eastern eyes: Cultural studies in the Gospels*. Downers Grove, IL: InterVarsity Press.

Galli, M. (2006). *Jesus mean and wild: The unexpected love of an untamable God*. Grand Rapids, MI: Baker Books.

Kimball, D. (2007). *They like Jesus but not the church: Insights from emerging generations*. Grand Rapids, MI: Zondervan.

Scazzero, P. (2006). *Emotionally healthy spirituality: It's impossible to be spiritually mature while remaining emotionally immature*. Grand Rapids, MI: Zondervan.

Sweet, L. (2014). *Me and we: God's new social gospel*. Nashville, TN: Abingdon Press.

Sweet, L. (2010). *Nudge: Awakening each other to the God who's already there*. Colorado Springs, CO: David C. Cook.

Tett, G. (2015). *The silo effect: The peril of expertise and the promise of breaking down barriers*. New York, NY: Simon & Schuster.

APA Essay Page 6

EXERCISES:

Exercise 23.1

Consider a writing assignment you will need to undertake in the near future. Prepare a sample title page using APA format. Take care to ensure that all components are accurate, and be creative with your title.

Exercise 23.2

Consider an assignment you have completed recently or an assignment you will undertake in the near future. Prepare a proper APA abstract page, taking care to follow all required components.

Exercise 23.3

Gather at least 10 sources for an assignment you have completed recently or an assignment you will undertake in the near future. Prepare a proper APA references page, taking care to list individual sources appropriately.

CHAPTER 24.

MLA

DEFINITION TO REMEMBER:

- **MLA = Modern Language Association** (typically used for liberal arts and humanities)

RULES TO REMEMBER:

1. Use 12 point, Times New Roman font, with 1" margins on all sides.
2. Include a header that numbers all pages consecutively in the upper right-hand corner, one half inch from the top of the page.
3. Your essay includes 2 main sections: body and works cited page. Do not include a title page unless your instructor specifically requests one.

SAMPLE PAPER:

Sample Paper in text-based format https://goo.gl/uX9TcH

Dr. Jennie A. Harrop

Professor Roger Nam

DMIN 726

26 April 2016

DMIN726 Academic Essay: From Missional to Meaningful

In his 2010 book *Nudge: Awakening Each Other to the God Who's Already There*, Leonard Sweet argues for a new kind of evangelism:

> The church has been more prone to "take a stand" on issues or "take a vote" on programs than touch. Touch is a centripetal force that includes and embraces. Taking stands is a centrifugal force that separates and divides. While the rest of the world is moving, the one taking a stand is frozen in time like kids playing freeze tag, waiting for the sign that says it's okay to move again. Christ ran around touching people and tagging them. Every Jesus tag offered freedom. Every Jesus tag let the person tagged know they had been touched by God. (242)

The Pharisees operated by centrifugal force; Jesus perpetuates a centripetal force. As a church, we know this, and yet our efforts to stand for truth in the twenty-first century invariably repel rather than attract. According to Dan Kimball, we are at a point where we need to offer both an apology and an apologetic: "While we need to stand strong on what we believe and need not be ashamed of the gospel in any way, we need to make sure we are presenting a biblical picture of the church and not perpetuating negative stereotypes. We need to offer an apologetic to correct misperceptions" (250). The earliest roots of the missional movement, which has been a direct attempt to rescript our ecclesiastical centrifugal spin into an inclusive centripetal force, began with conversations in the early twentieth century about missionary methods that were deemed

MLA Essay Page 1

too reliant on western superiority (Aniol). As this healthy look at missionary ecclesiology spread, writers/theologians such as Darrell Guder, Ed Stetzer, Tim Keller, and Alan Hirsch carried the conversation into a broader church context in the late twentieth century, calling for a missional church. And while I agree with the end goal of the missional approach, I believe the movement will eventually fade away without a direct and intentional articulation of (1) emotional quotient (EQ) and (2) audience quotient (AQ).

As Sweet argues in *Me and We: God's New Social Gospel,* the world's structural problems will remain as long as the individual human heart is ailing: "The [social gospel] movement's demise has been the subject of vast speculation and scrutiny, but it can be seen perhaps best this way: social gospelers tried to save an ailing turtle by switching out its shell, one embossed with the name 'Christianity'" (3). The missional movement is in danger of a similar end. If we don't pause in our discussion of the core ideas of missiology to consider how individual hearts can be strengthened and encouraged, missional ideas will never rise from rhetoric to reality. According to Gillian Tett, understanding the "messy gaps between rhetoric and reality" is critical: "Life does not always fit into the official descriptions of what people are *supposed* to do. Much of the time we ignore these messy realities" (224). How, then, do we ensure that our discussion of missional church adequately prepares, equips, and strengthens the hearts of those who are sent to disciple? Are we embarking on missions – both around the globe and across the street – without properly training disciples? Peter Scazzero writes that a healthy understanding of self is essential: "The vast majority of us go to our graves without knowing who we are. We unconsciously live someone else's life, or at least someone else's expectations for us. This does violence to ourselves, our relationship with God, and ultimately others" (66). In

MLA Essay Page 2

an effort to extend the missional conversation and keep the movement alive, an examination of individual EQ and AQ is an essential next step.

A Scriptural Shift

The scriptural underpinnings of the missional movement rest primarily in the Great Commission: "Then Jesus came to [the disciples] and said, 'All authority in heaven and on earth has been given to me. Therefore go and make disciples of all nations, baptizing them in the name of the Father and of the Son and of the Holy Spirit, and teaching them to obey everything I have commanded you. And surely I am with you always, to the very end of the age'" (*New International Version*, Matt. 28:18-20). But two problems are confronting us as we try to live into Jesus' commissioning: (1) We don't fully believe in our own authority and ability to do what Jesus is asking of us, and (2) We don't understand how to effectively speak to "all nations." In other words, while our godly purpose may make sense to us intellectually, we aren't properly equipped to live into it. As Mark Galli argues in *Jesus Mean and Wild: The Unexpected Love of an Untamable God,* when we begin to rationalize Jesus, we render the Great Commission vacuous and ineffective:

> We avoid the reality of Christ's power in a number of ways. For instance, we're tempted to spiritualize his power, to reduce the elemental potency and energy to a moment of personal religious inspiration. The stilling of the storm is about psychological storms in our lives. The healing of the lame is about solving emotional problems that cripple us. Jesus bringing sight to the blind is about God's ability to help us see our lives clearly. And so on and so forth. If we do that enough, we begin to think the Gospel stories are nothing but metaphors, and metaphors primarily about us." (113)

How do we rescue Jesus' meaning "from the barnacles that have attached themselves to it over the centuries"? (Bailey 343).

Works Cited

Aniol, Richard. "A Brief History of the Missional Church Movement." *Religious Affections Ministries*. Web. 23 April 2016.

Bailey, Kenneth E. *Jesus Through Middle Eastern Eyes: Cultural Studies in the Gospels*. Downers Grove, IL: InterVarsity Press, 2008. Print.

The Bible. New International Version, Zondervan, 1999.

Galli, Mark. *Jesus Mean and Wild: The Unexpected Love of an Untamable God*. Grand Rapids, MI: Baker Books, 2006. Print.

Kimball, Dan. *They Like Jesus but not the Church: Insights from Emerging Generations*. Grand Rapids, MI: Zondervan, 2007. Print.

Scazzero, Peter. *Emotionally Healthy Spirituality: It's Impossible to be Spiritually Mature While Remaining Emotionally Immature*. Grand Rapids, MI: Zondervan, 2006. Print.

Sweet, Leonard. *Me and We: God's New Social Gospel*. Nashville, TN: Abingdon Press, 2014.

Sweet, Leonard. *Nudge: Awakening Each Other to the God Who's Already There*. Colorado Springs, CO: David C. Cook, 2010. Print.

Tett, Gillian. *The Silo Effect: The Peril of Expertise and the Promise of Breaking Down Barriers*. New York, NY: Simon & Schuster, 2015. Print.

MLA Essay Page 5

EXERCISES:

Exercise 24.1

Consider a writing assignment you will need to undertake in the near future. Prepare a sample first page of an MLA essay. Take care to ensure that all components are accurate, and be creative with your title.

Exercise 24.2

Consider an assignment you have completed recently or an assignment you will undertake in the near future, and select a specific source for that assignment. Prepare a proper MLA summary, paraphrase, and direct quote using that source, taking care to follow all MLA parenthetical requirements precisely.

1. Summary:
2. Paraphrase:
3. Direct Quote:

Exercise 24.3

Gather at least 10 sources for an assignment you have completed recently or an assignment you will undertake in the near future. Prepare a proper MLA works cited page, taking care to list individual sources appropriately.

CHAPTER 25.

TURABIAN

DEFINITION TO REMEMBER:

- **Turabian formatting and The Chicago Manual of Style are essentially the same, with slight modifications in the latter** (both are typically used for liberal arts, humanities, and sciences)

RULES TO REMEMBER:

1. Use 12 point, Times New Roman font, with 1" margins on all sides.
2. Include a header that numbers all pages consecutively in the upper right-hand corner, one half inch from the top of the page.
3. Your essay includes 3 main sections: title page, body, and bibliography. If your instructor requires endnotes instead of footnotes, you will include an endnotes page in the back matter.

SAMPLE PAPER:

Essay file in text-based format https://goo.gl/g1z9ma

DMIN726 Academic Essay:

From Missional to Meaningful

Dr. Jennie A. Harrop

DMIN726: Dynamics of Leadership

April 26, 2016

In his 2010 book *Nudge: Awakening Each Other to the God Who's Already There*, Leonard Sweet argues for a new kind of evangelism:

> The church has been more prone to "take a stand" on issues or "take a vote" on programs than touch. Touch is a centripetal force that includes and embraces. Taking stands is a centrifugal force that separates and divides. While the rest of the world is moving, the one taking a stand is frozen in time like kids playing freeze tag, waiting for the sign that says it's okay to move again. Christ ran around touching people and tagging them. Every Jesus tag offered freedom. Every Jesus tag let the person tagged know they had been touched by God.[1]

The Pharisees operated by centrifugal force; Jesus perpetuates a centripetal force. As a church, we know this, and yet our efforts to stand for truth in the twenty-first century invariably repel rather than attract. According to Dan Kimball, we are at a point where we need to offer both an apology and an apologetic: "While we need to stand strong on what we believe and need not be ashamed of the gospel in any way, we need to make sure we are presenting a biblical picture of the church and not perpetuating negative stereotypes. We need to offer an apologetic to correct misperceptions."[2] The earliest roots of the missional movement, which has been a direct attempt to rescript our ecclesiastical centrifugal spin into an inclusive centripetal force, began with conversations in the early twentieth century about missionary methods that were deemed too reliant on western superiority.[3] As this healthy look at missionary ecclesiology spread, writers/theologians such as Darrell Guder, Ed Stetzer, Tim Keller, and Alan Hirsch carried the conversation into a broader church context in the late twentieth century, calling for a missional church. And while I agree with the end goal of the missional approach, I believe the movement

---

1. Leonard Sweet, *Nudge: Awakening Each Other to the God Who's Already There* (Colorado Springs, CO: David C. Cook, 2010), 242.

2. Dan Kimball, *They Like Jesus but not the Church: Insights from Emerging Generations* (Grand Rapids, MI: Zondervan, 2007), 250.

3. Scott Aniol, "A Brief History of the Missional Church Movement," *Religious Affections Ministries*, accessed April 23, 2016, http://religiousaffections.org/articles/articles-on-church/a-brief-history-of-the-missional-church-movement/.

Turabian Essay Page 2

will eventually fade away without a direct and intentional articulation of (1) emotional quotient (EQ) and (2) audience quotient (AQ).

As Sweet argues in *Me and We: God's New Social Gospel*, the world's structural problems will remain as long as the individual human heart is ailing: "The [social gospel] movement's demise has been the subject of vast speculation and scrutiny, but it can be seen perhaps best this way: social gospelers tried to save an ailing turtle by switching out its shell, one embossed with the name 'Christianity.'"[4] The missional movement is in danger of a similar end. If we don't pause in our discussion of the core ideas of missiology to consider how individual hearts can be strengthened and encouraged, missional ideas will never rise from rhetoric to reality. According to Gillian Tett, understanding the "messy gaps between rhetoric and reality" is critical: "Life does not always fit into the official descriptions of what people are *supposed* to do. Much of the time we ignore these messy realities."[5] How, then, do we ensure that our discussion of missional church adequately prepares, equips, and strengthens the hearts of those who are sent to disciple? Are we embarking on missions – both around the globe and across the street – without properly training disciples? Peter Scazzero writes that a healthy understanding of self is essential: "The vast majority of us go to our graves without knowing who we are. We unconsciously live someone else's life, or at least someone else's expectations for us. This does violence to ourselves, our relationship with God, and ultimately others."[6] In an effort to extend the missional conversation and keep the movement alive, an examination of individual EQ and AQ is an essential next step.

---

4. Leonard Sweet, *Me and We: God's New Social Gospel* (Nashville, TN: Abingdon Press, 2014), 3.

5. Gillian Tett, *The Silo Effect: The Peril of Expertise and the Promise of Breaking Down Barriers* (New York, NY: Simon & Schuster, 2015), 224.

6. Peter Scazzero, *Emotionally Healthy Spirituality: It's Impossible to be Spiritually Mature While Remaining Emotionally Immature,* (Grand Rapids, MI: Zondervan, 2006) 66.

Turabian Essay Page 3

A Scriptural Shift

The scriptural underpinnings of the missional movement rest primarily in the Great Commission: "Then Jesus came to [the disciples] and said, 'All authority in heaven and on earth has been given to me. Therefore go and make disciples of all nations, baptizing them in the name of the Father and of the Son and of the Holy Spirit, and teaching them to obey everything I have commanded you. And surely I am with you always, to the very end of the age.'"[7] But two problems are confronting us as we try to live into Jesus' commissioning: (1) We don't fully believe in our own authority and ability to do what Jesus is asking of us, and (2) We don't understand how to effectively speak to "all nations." In other words, while our godly purpose may make sense to us intellectually, we aren't properly equipped to live into it. As Mark Galli argues in *Jesus Mean and Wild: The Unexpected Love of an Untamable God,* when we begin to rationalize Jesus, we render the Great Commission vacuous and ineffective:

> We avoid the reality of Christ's power in a number of ways. For instance, we're tempted to spiritualize his power, to reduce the elemental potency and energy to a moment of personal religious inspiration. The stilling of the storm is about psychological storms in our lives. The healing of the lame is about solving emotional problems that cripple us. Jesus bringing sight to the blind is about God's ability to help us see our lives clearly. And so on and so forth. If we do that enough, we begin to think the Gospel stories are nothing but metaphors, and metaphors primarily about us."[8]

How do we rescue Jesus' meaning "from the barnacles that have attached themselves to it over the centuries"?[9]

---

7. Matt. 28:18-20 (NIV).

8. Mark Galli, *Jesus Mean and Wild: The Unexpected Love of an Untamable God* (Grand Rapids, MI: Baker Books, 2006), 113.

9. Kenneth E. Bailey, *Jesus Through Middle Eastern Eyes: Cultural Studies in the Gospels* (Downers Grove, IL: InterVarsity Press, 2008), 343.

Turabian Essay Page 4

Bibliography

Aniol, Richard. "A Brief History of the Missional Church Movement." *Religious Affections Ministries*. Accessed April 23, 2016. http://religiousaffections.org/articles/articles-on-church/a-brief-history-of-the-missional-church-movement/

Bailey, Kenneth E. *Jesus Through Middle Eastern Eyes: Cultural Studies in the Gospels*. Downers Grove, IL: InterVarsity Press, 2008.

Galli, Mark. *Jesus Mean and Wild: The Unexpected Love of an Untamable God*. Grand Rapids, MI: Baker Books, 2006.

Kimball, Dan. *They Like Jesus but not the Church: Insights from Emerging Generations*. Grand Rapids, MI: Zondervan, 2007.

Scazzero, Peter. *Emotionally Healthy Spirituality: It's Impossible to be Spiritually Mature While Remaining Emotionally Immature*. Grand Rapids, MI: Zondervan, 2006.

Sweet, Leonard. *Me and We: God's New Social Gospel*. Nashville, TN: Abingdon Press, 2014.

-----. *Nudge: Awakening Each Other to the God Who's Already There*. Colorado Springs, CO: David C. Cook, 2010.

Tett, Gillian. *The Silo Effect: The Peril of Expertise and the Promise of Breaking Down Barriers*. New York, NY: Simon & Schuster, 2015.

Turabian Essay Page 5

EXERCISES:

Exercise 25.1

Consider a writing assignment you will need to undertake in the near future. Prepare a sample title page using Turabian format. Take care to ensure that all components are accurate, and be creative with your title.

Exercise 25.2

Consider an assignment you have completed recently or an assignment you will undertake in the near future, and select a specific source for that assignment. Prepare a proper Turabian summary, paraphrase, and direct quote using that source, taking care to follow all Turabian footnote or endnote requirements precisely.

1. Summary:
2. Paraphrase:
3. Direct Quote:

Exercise 25.3

Gather at least 10 sources for an assignment you have completed recently or an assignment you will undertake in the near future. Prepare a proper Turabian bibliography, taking care to list individual sources appropriately.

PART VII.

BEYOND ACADEMIA

Many students assume that concepts like effective thesis statements and the sentence, paragraph, and essay equations are specific to scholarly work only, but that is not the case. Everything we have covered in this text applies to the writing we do daily in our personal and work lives. When you compose a text, the better you understand your purpose and audience, the less likely your recipient is to respond with a "??" If you write an email to your child's teacher about a volatile concern, the more tightly you hold to the topic sentence + evidence structure, the more likely you are to be heard well. When you compose an email of inquiry to a prospective employer, your ability to reproduce an introduction + body paragraphs + conclusion format is likely to receive a favorable response. Our brains are wired for an expected linguistic structure, and the better you hold to the simple math, the more effectively you will be able to communicate your purpose.

CHAPTER 26.

EMAILS

Much as our body language makes an impression when we walk into a room, the structure, content, and intent of our email can have an immediate impact on the recipient – whether we intend it or not. [Image: Samuel Zeller | Unsplash]

While email communication is convenient and efficient, we sometimes forget the effect that our words have on others. Much as our body language makes an impression when we walk into a room, the structure, content, and intent of our email can have an immediate impact on the recipient – whether we intend it or not. For every email you write, consider the following:

1. **Select an appropriate email address.** While a snarky, sardonic address may seem amusing at the time, an unprofessional name will often leave an impression you do not intend. Employers have said they are for more likely to favor a standard johnsmith@yahoo address over something like drunkensquirl@gmail or hizzyfit03@comcast. Choose wisely.

> "My email may be the first impression that I make on someone. I always check my emails before I send; is my writing reflecting the person I want them to see?" *Tori Ruiz, Executive Assistant to the Vice President for Student Life, Willamette University*

2. **Know your audience.** If you are sending an email to someone you don't yet know or someone you don't know well, the responsibility is yours to do a little research. Are you able to track down the person's age, gender, job title, education, location, and outside interests? The more you know, the better you will be able to speak directly to your audience.
3. **Know your purpose.** Before you write, ask yourself if you are able to state the purpose of your email in a single sentence or less. If not, keep pondering until you are. The evidence to support your ideas may take longer than a single sentence, but your key purpose should always be stated simply and succinctly.
4. **Title the subject line appropriately.** The subject line often is the first impression your audience has, and that impression can be reinforced again and again as the email

conversation continues. When you have an inadvertent typo or an uninspired word in the subject line, you will see it repeated until the conversation abates – as will your audience.

5. **Introduce yourself.** Do not assume that your email address or final signature will suffice. Allow your audience the courtesy of a quick reminder of who you are, just as you might remind someone of your name and association in a social setting.
6. **Keep it concise and clear.** Many of us have known friends or coworkers whose emails we dread – not because they are unkind but because they prattle on and on without landing on a singular point. Don't be that person. Once you have articulated your purpose, hold to the simple math for an effective paragraph – topic sentence + evidence – or, if appropriate, the simple math for an effective essay.
7. **Keep it professional.** Begin with a salutation (Dear Ms. Wilson or Mr. Amos), continue with your main points, avoid text-inspired abbreviations, and maintain a respectful tone throughout.
8. **Monitor your emotions.** While we have all occasionally received irritating or even infuriating emails, the beauty of the medium is that an immediate response is typically not required. If you feel your emotions getting the best of you, step away from the email until you have time to get a little perspective. Taking a little extra time can be the healthiest approach for both you and your audience.
9. **Include a professional signature.** If you don't yet have an email signature, create one. Rather than a *dash + first name* approach, a consistent signature with your full name and title will leave an impression of professionalism, authority, and attention to detail.
10. **Maintain privacy.** Only discuss public matters in an email, and be careful about adding others to the conversation without first asking permission. An inadvertent *reply all*

when you intended only *reply* can be enough to sabotage your reputation for years to come. Just as you would pay keen attention to social boundaries in a face-to-face meeting, be aware of those boundaries in email discussions as well.
11. **Avoid one-liners.** While it can be tempting to respond with a simple *Sure* or *Thanks*, be careful about dipping into one-line responses when your audience may find them flippant or disrespectful. Always allow the audience member with the most authority to begin the one-liner relationship first, ensuring that no one will be offended by a step in the direction of mere efficiency.
12. **Respond in a timely manner.** The efficiency of email allows for conversations to move continually forward, ideally progressing toward a new decision or action. When the email is in your inbox, don't keep others waiting any longer than you must. You will be judged for your ability to keep things moving forward.

EXERCISES:

Exercise 26.1

Locate an email you have sent recently for a school or work-related situation. Consider your email in light of each of the following standards. How does it fare?

1. Select an appropriate email address.
2. Know your audience.
3. Know your purpose.
4. Title the subject line appropriately.
5. Introduce yourself.
6. Keep it concise and clear.
7. Keep it professional.

8. Monitor your emotions.
9. Include a professional signature.
10. Maintain privacy.

Exercise 26.2

Find an email you have received from someone else for a school or work-related situation. Weigh the email in light of each of the following standards. How does it fare?

1. Select an appropriate email address.
2. Know your audience.
3. Know your purpose.
4. Title the subject line appropriately.
5. Introduce yourself.
6. Keep it concise and clear.
7. Keep it professional.
8. Monitor your emotions.
9. Include a professional signature.
10. Maintain privacy.

Exercise 26.3

Consider something you hope to accomplish or change. To whom should you write an email to get a conversation started? Should you address the email to more than one person? Write the email according to the standards listed in this chapter.

CHAPTER 27.

LETTERS

The purpose of any business letter is to persuade an audience to think differently, take action, or consider change. What claim will you make and what appeals will you use to persuade your audience? [Image: Mathyas Kurmann | Unsplash]

While email is a convenient and efficient way to communicate, the business letter is still a preferred form of communication in more formal situations. When you write a business letter, whether you send it through the postal mail or as an email attachment, be sure to hold to the following expected standards:

1. **Know your purpose.** Are you writing to inform, persuade, entertain, or remind your audience? Are you able to state your purpose in a single sentence? What evidence will you provide to support your single-sentence purpose? How will you ensure that your letter holds to the simple math of *topic sentence + evidence = paragraph* and *introduction + body paragraphs + conclusion = essay*?

> "I'm often self-conscious of how my email could come across. I never want it to be, or sound, intimidating. I've decided if I can include a lot of '!!!' or ':)' then it'll quickly break that mold. But then again, I wonder if I am breaking some type of writing rule. :)" *Emily Call, Associate Director of Admissions*

2. **Know your audience.** If you aren't sure what your audience looks like, lives like, or sounds like, do the necessary research until you have a better sense. A blind letter written to a general audience will rarely achieve what its writer intends. Do your homework; it will always pay off.
3. **Select a professional letterhead.** Years ago, employees were reliant on their employer for permission to use the company letterhead. And while professional etiquette still suggests that you seek permission before usurping someone else's design or name, feel free to create your own. A simple design using your initials or last name can mean the difference between a letter that appears homemade and

poorly planned and a letter that is professional, confident, and compelling.

4. **Use a standard format and font**. A business letter is typically in 12 point Times New Roman or Cambria font, with 1" margins, single-spaced except for extra spaces between paragraphs, and presented in a block format:

SAMPLE LETTER:

Sample Letter in text-based format https://goo.gl/DXrUWv

Sample Business Letter

5. **Be professional.** Avoid text-inspired abbreviations, personal topics, and emotional outbursts. Instead maintain a keen sense of purpose, audience, voice, and clarity.
6. **Write clearly and succinctly.** A business letter is not the time for lengthy stories, lead-ins, or discussions. State your purpose, provide your evidence, and suggest further action or communication. Save the longer discussions for an in-person visit.
7. **Be persuasive.** Keep in mind that the purpose of any business letter is to persuade an audience to think differently, take action, or consider change. What claim will you make and what appeals will you use to persuade your audience? What evidence will you provide to support your claim? How will you ensure that your voice is both humble and authoritative, open-minded and confident?
8. **Expect a response.** Every business letter should end with a call to action, whether that call is for further discussion, a different direction, or even just a new line of thinking. How will your letter request a response without sounding presumptuous or overbearing? How can you present yourself in such a way that your audience is intrigued by your ideas and interested in future considerations?

EXERCISES:

Exercise 27.1

Locate a business letter you have sent and consider it in light of each of the following standards. How does it fare?

1. Know your purpose.
2. Know your audience.
3. Select a professional letterhead.
4. Use a standard format and font.

5. Be professional.
6. Write clearly and succinctly.
7. Be persuasive.
8. Expect a response.

Exercise 27.2

Find a business letter you have received from someone else for a school or work-related situation. Weigh the letter in light of each of the following standards. How does it fare?

1. Know your purpose.
2. Know your audience.
3. Select a professional letterhead.
4. Use a standard format and font.
5. Be professional.
6. Write clearly and succinctly.
7. Be persuasive.
8. Expect a response.

Exercise 27.3

Consider something you hope to accomplish or change. To whom should you write a business letter to get a conversation started? Should you address the letter to more than one person? Write the letter according to the standards listed in this chapter.

CHAPTER 28.

REPORTS AND PROPOSALS

A business proposal is not just about persuasion. Embedded in any effective proposal is a new way of doing that may demand change and risk. [Image: Benjamin Child | Unsplash]

Like emails and business letters, reports and proposals are also a regular part of business writing in the work world, and any educated adult should feel at ease with proposing new ideas in writing. As with all effective writing, keep your audience, purpose, and voice at the forefront, and all should go well.

1. **Analyze your audience.** If you intend to propose something new, don't just assume you *know* your audience; *analyze* them. Consider their age, location, education, employment, class, race, gender, religion, motivation, and interests. What do they think about, dream about, care about? What can you offer them that they don't already know about or realize? Why will they listen to you?
2. **Know your purpose.** In a sentence, what are you proposing and why? How do you hope your audience will think differently about life after reading your work? How is your purpose unique and essential? How will you teach your audience a new way of thinking?
3. **Articulate a methodology.** A business proposal is not just about persuasion. Embedded in any

> "One of the most valuable classes I took in college was 'Business Communication.' We learned about writing professional emails, memos, and letters. I remember the professor telling us that when they surveyed local employers, business writing was one of the areas that had the most impact. I use the content and skills from that class more in my daily work than some of the subject matter from my major! Effective communication is crucial to what I do and has helped me to establish myself in the workplace." *Megan Janes, Associate Director of Graduate and Adult Degree Admissions*

effective proposal is a new way of doing that may demand change and risk. What new methods are you proposing, and how will your audience adopt and apply those new methods? What learning curve do you anticipate, and how will the information be shared in a way that is consistent, uniform, and transformative?

4. **Ponder a solution.** What will be the end result? If your audience invests in the changes you are proposing, what can they expect to see and experience? Will a solution be evident immediately, or will it demand time, patience, and endurance?

5. **Consider the competition.** Just as an effective argument must weigh opposing arguments, a successful business proposal must weigh the competition. What other options does your audience have, and why is your approach the most logical, meaningful, promising, and inspiring? Are there downfalls about the competition that your audience might not know, and are there benefits that you are asking them to overlook? Why?

6. **Be professional.** Platitudes and generalities are not helpful in a business proposal. If you hope to form a relationship built on trust, focus your proposal on the specific qualities that will foster a mutual understanding. How can you ensure your audience that you are knowledgeable and trustworthy?

7. **Be persuasive.** What will convince your audience to listen to your ideas? Will you use appeals of reason, emotion, or character? What evidence will you employ to demonstrate the truth of what you are suggesting? What data supports your cause? How will your voice, syntax, and diction aid in persuading your audience? How will the visual and mixed media components of your proposal strengthen your cause? What holes remain in your argument, and what will you do to fill them?

8. **Use a standard format and font.** As with a business letter,

the general standard is to hold to a basic font and layout: 12 point Times New Roman with 1" margins and clean, easy-to-read paragraphs or lists. What visuals will you include to ensure that your presentation is eye-catching and professional but not sloppy or distracting? Should you purchase software created specifically for business proposals and reports?

9. **Edit carefully.** A single error in the simple math of the sentence, paragraph, or essay is enough to destroy the trust you are hoping to build with a potential new partner. How will you ensure that your work is error-free?

10. **Expect a response.** Does your writing exude the confidence of someone who expects a positive result? How do you demonstrate to your audience that you are knowledgeable, authoritative, and confident? If you are the best in your field, how does that show in the words you have written in your proposal?

EXERCISES:

Exercise 28.1

Locate a business proposal you have prepared and consider it in light of each of the following standards. How does it fare?

1. Analyze your audience.
2. Know your purpose.
3. Articulate a methodology.
4. Ponder a solution.
5. Consider the competition.
6. Be professional.
7. Be persuasive.
8. Use a standard format and font.
9. Edit carefully.

10. Expect a response.

Exercise 28.2

Find a business proposal you have received from someone else for a school or work-related situation. Weigh the proposal in light of each of the following standards. How does it fare?

1. Analyze your audience.
2. Know your purpose.
3. Articulate a methodology.
4. Ponder a solution.
5. Consider the competition.
6. Be professional.
7. Be persuasive.
8. Use a standard format and font.
9. Edit carefully.
10. Expect a response.

Exercise 28.3

Consider something you hope to accomplish or change. To whom should you write a business proposal to get a conversation started? Write the proposal according to the standards listed in this chapter.

CONCLUSION

Effective communication with the world around us begins with intentionality.
[Image: Slava Bowman | Unsplash]

When we talk about writing, three kinds of responses typically arise:

1. **Fear**
    - What if I sound stupid?
    - What if I can't get my ideas from my head to the screen/page?
    - I'm just guessing, and I always guess incorrectly.

- Other people understand the rules, but I'm just no good at it.

2. **Ambivalence**

    - Why does it matter where my commas are, as long as I say what I mean?
    - Who cares about grammar when the important thing is getting my ideas out there?
    - The rules are always changing anyway, so why bother?

    The English language has so many exceptions to the rules that no one can really learn it all anyway.

3. **Inattention**

    - I don't have time to read. I need to keep things moving.
    - Why would I bother to rethink what I've already said?
    - Rules are for other people.
    - What errors?

In the pre-internet world of the late 20th century, our fear of permanence froze our fingers over the keyboard or holding the pencil, as if the words that emerged would somehow be cemented to our reputation. Now that our 21st-century words hover permanently in cyberspace – something we never would have believed just a few short decades ago – we seem to have lost our social filters as we like, friend, critique, affirm, and shame one another in a global format.

Somewhere between anxiety and narcissism lies a middle ground where the rules are necessary for us to communicate well. English, beautifully infused with myriad languages from its immigrant peoples, is one of the most nuanced languages in the world. Each punctuation mark inspires emotional responses, whether conscious or subconscious, and a misplaced comma or inadvertent dash can lead to misunderstandings both fleeting and permanent.

Mechanics matter, and the rules are simple. Once we recognize the simple math, we can replace the fear, ambivalence, and inattention with **intentionality**. And with intentionality comes the freedom of knowing that our words will connect us clearly and confidently with the world around us.

ABOUT THE AUTHOR

Dr. Jennie A. Harrop is a professor in George Fox University's Department of Professional Studies, where she teaches writing, literature, and Christian apologetics, and serves as department chair. She holds a PhD in English from the University of Denver, an MFA in creative writing from Colorado State University, and a BA in journalism from Pacific Lutheran University, and she is completing a Doctor of Ministry in Semiotics and Future Studies at Portland Seminary. In addition to her teaching and administrative duties at George Fox, Harrop serves as director of the university's Portland Writing Center. She lives in Oregon with her husband and five children.

Made in the USA
Monee, IL
12 January 2021